EVERY DAY I PRAY for My Teenager

Eastman Curtis

Charisma
HOUSE
A STRANG COMPANY

EVERY DAY I PRAY FOR MY TEENAGER by Eastman Curtis
Published by Charisma House
A Strang Company
600 Rinehart Road
Lake Mary, FL 32746
www.charismahouse.com

Unless otherwise noted, all Scripture quotations are from the Holy Bible,
New International Version. Copyright © 1973, 1978, 1984,
International Bible Society. Used by permission.

Scripture quotations marked AMP are from the Amplified Bible.
Old Testament copyright © 1965, 1987 by the Zondervan Corporation.
The Amplified New Testament copyright © 1954, 1958, 1987 by
the Lockman Foundation. Used by permission.

Scripture quotations marked KJV are from the King James
Version of the Bible.

Scripture quotations marked NKJV are from the
New King James Version of the Bible. Copyright © 1979, 1980,
1982 by Thomas Nelson, Inc., publishers. Used by permission.

Illustrations in the book by Beth Thomas

Library of Congress Catalog Card Number: 96-85028
International Standard Book Number: 0-88419-435-3

03 04 05 06 — 15 14 13 12
Printed in the United States of America

This book is dedicated to all parents who want to pray
and make a difference in their teenagers' lives
and ultimately in all of our futures.

And to our own blessings, Sumner and Nicole,
who continue to bring joy and adventure to our lives.

Acknowledgments

Special thanks to our parents. Because of their prayers and the supply of the Holy Spirit we continue to run the race — Dad and Mom, it works!

Also to Chuck E. Tate and Sarah Bruzelius for all of your constructive input. We couldn't have done it without you.

To Utuana Graham for your faithful dedication to the call of this ministry. We love you.

As well as to the staff at Creation House for your support and commitment to see the gospel spread to all ages.

CONTENTS

SECTION I
SPIRITUAL LIFE

SECTION II
BONDAGE-BREAKING
PRAYERS

SECTION III
RELATIONSHIPS

SECTION IV
SCHOOL NEEDS

SECTION V
LIFE SKILLS

Please note that this book alternates between use of the
masculine voice and the feminine voice in the prayers.

MEET EASTMAN CURTIS

Eastman Curtis is a dynamic communicator of the gospel of Jesus Christ! His heartbeat is to bring people into their divine destiny. With an attitude for excellence, Eastman uses every venue possible to share his message.

He has authored several books and is a columnist in many Christian periodicals. His zeal for God and America's teens has extended over national airwaves in his television series *This Generation* as well as a thirty-minute special aired by FOX affiliates titled *Eastman Curtis Live.* Eastman has also produced a series of ninety-second radio devotionals that have been enjoyed by audiences nationwide for their practical and humorous teachings on real-life issues.

Eastman also hosts twenty life-changing weekend crusades each year for teenagers and youth leaders called This Generation Conventions. Whether preaching at churches, business meetings or conventions, he communicates the message of hope in Christ with relevance and integrity, making him one of the most sought-after speakers in America.

Eastman Curtis Ministries is located in Tulsa, Oklahoma, where he and his wife, Angel, are raising their son, Sumner, and daughter, Nicole.

INTRODUCTION

In the time it takes you to read this introduction, approximately 294 teenagers will have dropped out of high school, 125 teenagers will lose their virginity, and 83 teenagers will smoke their first cigarette. By the end of today these numbers will increase to 14,000, 6,000 and 4,000 respectively. Statistics like these give voice to the volatile times our teenagers live in and more than just cause for us as parents to rise against this tidal wave of deception with the most powerful force we have: prayer!

God's master plan of redemption for our lives doesn't cover only forgiveness of sin, healing of our bodies and blessings in our finances. The Bible is full of redemptive promises for our children. It's sad that many of us parents have never taken full advantage of the great inheritance Jesus purchased for us and our children. If ever there was a time to understand and propitiate these promises, the time is now!

Get ready for results! This book is designed to be a tool and a resource for you, using the spiritual jurisdiction God has given you to help your teenager. Whether you are believing to protect them from falling into sin or believing to see them delivered from the bondage that may presently be holding them captive, the prayers in this book, when mixed with your faith in God, will bring about a dramatic change.

My own life is a testimony to the tremendous work prayer can accomplish. I was raised in a single-parent, non-Christian household. By the time I was seventeen I had been kicked out of three schools for substance abuse and the negative influence I had on others. But I had a grandmother who prayed for me. I am convinced now more than ever that God heard my grandmother's sustaining prayers and saw her unwavering faith which resulted in my salvation. I went from a drug-selling, campus flunky to an honor roll student. In fact I received the first full-ride scholarship offered to anyone at my boarding school for my leadership capabilities and exemplary conduct! If God did this for me, He will do it for anyone.

For the past eighteen years I have dedicated my life to ministering to teenagers and their parents, conducting conventions and church meetings all over this nation, Asia, South America and Europe. Because of my radical experience with Jesus Christ at the age of seventeen, I have always had a consuming desire to see our teenagers serve the Lord with all their hearts. As you pray these scriptural prayers for your teenager and study the accompanying Bible verses you will discover the crucial role God has predestined teenagers to play in this end-time revival.

> In the last days, God says, I will pour out my Spirit on all people. Your sons and daughters will prophesy (Acts 2:17).

In 1992 the Lord, through His Holy Spirit, told me a revival was coming among American teenagers such as has never been seen in the history of humanity. I believe we as parents have a part to play in igniting the spark that will initiate this next great move of God! This book of Bible-based prayers will make a tremendous difference in your teenagers' lives if you will pray for them in faith. You have God's Word on it!

We don't have to sit back and passively watch our teenagers be taken captive by the devil. You hold in your hand a powerful tool that will thwart every evil plan the enemy has for your children — prayer. The Amplified Bible says in James 5:16:

> The earnest (heartfelt, continued) prayer of a righteous man makes tremendous power available [dynamic in its working].

Prayer is power, and it changes things.

It doesn't matter how difficult your particular situation may seem. God is your very present help in this time of trouble! You don't have to stand back helplessly and hold your breath through the teen years. You can make the difference *through prayer.*

SECTION I

SPIRITUAL LIFE

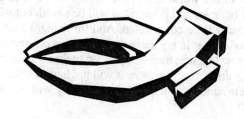

GOD'S WORD SAYS

1. "The promise is for you and your children and for all who are far off — for all whom the Lord our God will call" (Acts 2:39).

2. "In the last days, God says, I will pour out my Spirit on all people. Your sons and daughters will prophesy, your young men will see visions, your old men will dream dreams" (Acts 2:17).

3. "Jesus Christ is the same yesterday and today and forever" (Heb. 13:8).

4. "If you then, though you are evil, know how to give good gifts to your children, how much more will your Father in heaven give the Holy Spirit to those who ask him" (Luke 11:13).

5. "Go into all the world and preach the good news to all creation. Whoever believes and is baptized will be saved, but whoever does not believe will be condemned. And these signs will accompany those who believe: In my name they will drive out demons; they will speak in new tongues; they will pick up snakes with their hands; and when they drink deadly poison, it will not hurt them at all; they will place their hands on sick people, and they will get well" (Mark 16:15-18).

6. "Who is it that overcomes the world? Only he who believes that Jesus is the Son of God" (1 John 5:5).

7. "Come, all you who are thirsty, come to the waters; and you who have no money, come, buy and eat! Come, buy wine and milk without money and without cost" (Is. 55:1).

8. "On the last and greatest day of the Feast, Jesus stood and said in a loud voice, 'If anyone is thirsty, let him come to me and drink. Whoever believes in me, as the Scripture has said, streams of living water will flow from within him'" (John 7:37-38).

1

THE BAPTISM OF THE SPIRIT

Father, thank You that _____ is born-again and is a child of God. You have promised to pour out Your Holy Spirit in the last days for me, my children and all who are far off.[1] Your Spirit will enable our sons and daughters to do great exploits.[2] Thank You that You are the same God yesterday, today and forever.[3]

I know You desire to give good gifts to Your children,[4] and I am asking You to immerse my child in the power of the Holy Spirit. Equip him for service to be a world changer.[5] He is not overcome by the world but will overcome the world through the power of God.[6]

Cause my child to be thirsty for the things of God; to drink deeply from Your Spirit.[7] You said if anyone is thirsty let him come to You and drink, and out of his innermost being will flow rivers of living water. May rivers of God flow out of my child and bring life, healing and deliverance to everyone he comes in contact with.[8]

GOD'S WORD SAYS

1. "Before I formed you in the womb I knew you, before you were born I set you apart; I appointed you as a prophet to the nations" (Jer. 1:5).

2. "As for you, the anointing you received from him remains in you, and you do not need anyone to teach you. But as his anointing teaches you about all things and as that anointing is real, not counterfeit — just as it has taught you, remain in him" (1 John 2:27).

3. "But if I say, 'I will not mention him or speak any more in his name,' his word is in my heart like a fire, a fire shut up in my bones. I am weary of holding it in; indeed, I cannot" (Jer. 20:9).

4. "Have you not put a hedge around him and his household and everything he has? You have blessed the work of his hands, so that his flocks and herds are spread throughout the land" (Job 1:10).

5. "His divine power has given us everything we need for life and godliness through our knowledge of him who called us by his own glory and goodness" (2 Pet. 1:3).

6. "And God is able to make all grace abound to you, so that in all things at all times, having all that you need, you will abound in every good work" (2 Cor. 9:8).

7. "The path of the righteous is like the first gleam of dawn, shining ever brighter till the full light of day" (Prov. 4:18).

8. "The Spirit of the Lord is on me, because he has anointed me to preach good news to the poor. He has sent me to proclaim freedom for the prisoners and recovery of sight for the blind, to release the oppressed" (Luke 4:18).

9. "'Well done, good and faithful servant! You have been faithful with a few things; I will put you in charge of many things. Come and share your master's happiness!'"(Matt. 25:23).

2
THE CALL OF GOD

Father, thank You that before _____ was even born You knew her and had a plan for her life.[1] You have placed Your anointing upon her life.[2] I am asking You to burn Your call into her heart. Let it be as a fire shut up in her bones so she cannot hold it in.[3]

I pray a hedge of protection over my child so that no man, woman or enemy will squelch what You have in store for her.[4] You are equipping her with all things that pertain to life and godliness so that she will have an abundance for every good deed.[5]

Confirm Your call on her life by Your Spirit,[6] and make her path like the first gleam of dawn, shining ever brighter as she follows her calling.[7] Let multitudes of lives be touched by Your anointing which is flowing through her.[8] When she enters into Your kingdom, You will say, "Well done, good and faithful servant!"[9]

God's Word Says

1. "Through these he has given us his very great and precious promises, so that through them you may participate in the divine nature and escape the corruption in the world caused by evil desires" (2 Pet. 1:4).

2. "That is why I am suffering as I am. Yet I am not ashamed, because I know whom I have believed, and am convinced that he is able to guard what I have entrusted to him for that day" (2 Tim. 1:12).

3. "Who through faith are shielded by God's power until the coming of the salvation that is ready to be revealed in the last time" (1 Pet. 1:5).

4. "Love the Lord your God with all your heart and with all your soul and with all your mind and with all your strength" (Mark 12:30).

5. "For the word of God is living and active. Sharper than any double-edged sword, it penetrates even to dividing soul and spirit, joints and marrow; it judges the thoughts and attitudes of the heart" (Heb. 4:12).

6. "Do your best to present yourself to God as one approved, a workman who does not need to be ashamed and who correctly handles the word of truth" (2 Tim. 2:15).

7. "Come near to God and he will come near to you. Wash your hands, you sinners, and purify your hearts, you double-minded" (James 4:8).

8. "He who has an ear, let him hear what the Spirit says to the churches" (Rev. 2:7).

9. "Commit your way to the Lord; trust in him and he will do this" (Ps. 37:5).

3
CHRISTIAN COMMITMENT

Dear heavenly Father, I praise You for every one of Your great and precious promises to me and to my children.[1] Thank You for promising to keep and protect everything I have committed unto You until that day.[2] I commit _____ into Your loving hands right now by faith, knowing that You will guard him by the power of God unto salvation.[3] Give him an unquenchable desire to serve You with all his heart, soul, mind and strength.[4] Give him revelation out of Your Word which is sharper than any two-edged sword.[5] Thank You that he is using Your Word to break down any opposition that comes his way. I pray he will study to show himself approved unto You, a young man who needs not to be ashamed of You.[6]

I thank You, Father, that as he draws close to You, You will draw close to him.[7] Speak to him, I pray, and give him an ear to hear Your voice.[8] I thank You that he is committing his way unto You, and You are bringing his dreams to pass.[9] Keep him strong and committed to You. In Jesus' name!

GOD'S WORD SAYS

1. "The thief comes only to steal and kill and destroy; I have come that they may have life, and have it to the full" (John 10:10).

2. "Later Jesus found him at the temple and said to him, 'See, you are well again. Stop sinning or something worse may happen to you'" (John 5:14).

3. "You answer us with awesome deeds of righteousness, O God our Savior, the hope of all the ends of the earth and of the farthest seas" (Ps. 65:5).

4. It is better to take refuge in the Lord than to trust in man. It is better to take refuge in the Lord than to trust in princes" (Ps. 118:8-9).

5. "Like a bad tooth or a lame foot is reliance on the unfaithful in times of trouble" (Prov. 25:19).

6. "I can do everything through him who gives me strength" (Phil. 4:13).

7. "So do not throw away your confidence; it will be richly rewarded" (Heb. 10:35).

8. "In him and through faith in him we may approach God with freedom and confidence" (Eph. 3:12).

4

CONFIDENCE

Heavenly Father, I come before You today to thank You for my child. I praise You for giving her Your life.[1]

Give her supernatural confidence in You.[2] Start right now by building her esteem in You, for Your Word says that You are our confidence.[3] I pray that _____ will put her total confidence in You — not in others.[4] Even though others may be unfaithful and disappoint her, You will never let her down.[5] May she always remember that she can do all things through You, Jesus.[6]

Don't let her cast away her confidence,[7] but let her press forward in You. For by faith she can approach You with freedom and confidence.[8] In Jesus' name.

God's Word Says

1. "I am not saying this because I am in need, for I have learned to be content whatever the circumstances" (Phil. 4:11).

2. "But godliness with contentment is great gain" (1 Tim. 6:6).

3. "And I — in righteousness I will see your face; when I awake, I will be satisfied with seeing your likeness" (Ps. 17:15).

4. "Command those who are rich in this present world not to be arrogant nor to put their hope in wealth, which is so uncertain, but to put their hope in God, who richly provides us with everything for our enjoyment" (1 Tim. 6:17).

5. "Blessed are those who hunger and thirst for righteousness, for they will be filled" (Matt. 5:6).

6. "His master replied, 'Well done, good and faithful servant! You have been faithful with a few things; I will put you in charge of many things. Come and share your master's happiness!'" (Matt. 25:21).

5

CONTENTMENT

Heavenly Father, I lift up _____ to You. Thank You for loving him. Today I am asking You to cause my child to be content with the things which You have given to him at this time.[1] May he learn that contentment with godliness will produce great gain.[2] Let him find his contentment and satisfaction in You.[3] Cause him to see how futile it is to put his trust in material things, but let his hope be in You, who gives us richly all things to enjoy.[4]

God, cause my child to be consumed with a hunger and thirst for Your righteousness,[5] for You have promised to fill him. Make him faithful in the little things so that he will be blessed with much.[6] In Jesus' name.

GOD'S WORD SAYS

1. "Therefore, since we are surrounded by such a great cloud of witnesses, let us throw off everything that hinders and the sin that so easily entangles, and let us run with perseverance the race marked out for us. Let us fix our eyes on Jesus, the author and perfecter of our faith, who for the joy set before him endured the cross, scorning its shame, and sat down at the right hand of the throne of God" (Heb. 12:1-2).

2. "And afterward, I will pour out my Spirit on all people. Your sons and daughters will prophesy, your old men will dream dreams, your young men will see visions" (Joel 2:28).

3. "And the Lord answered me, and said, Write the vision, and make it plain upon tables, that he may run that readeth it" (Hab. 2:2, KJV).

4. "Do you not know that in a race all the runners run, but only one gets the prize? Run in such a way as to get the prize. Everyone who competes in the games goes into strict training. They do it to get a crown that will not last; but we do it to get a crown that will last forever. Therefore I do not run like a man running aimlessly; I do not fight like a man beating the air. No, I beat my body and make it my slave so that after I have preached to others, I myself will not be disqualified for the prize" (1 Cor. 9:24-27).

5. "Being confident of this, that he who began a good work in you will carry it on to completion until the day of Christ Jesus" (Phil. 1:6).

6. "Those who do wickedly against the covenant he shall corrupt with flattery; but the people who know their God shall be strong, and carry out great exploits" (Dan. 11:32, NKJV).

7. "For surely, O Lord, you bless the righteous; you surround them with your favor as with a shield" (Ps. 5:12).

6

DESTINY

Heavenly Father, thank You for the calling You have placed on _____ 's life. You have mapped out a course specifically for her. Thank You that she will be able to fulfill the destiny You have for her as she perseveres.[1]

You promised to pour out Your Spirit upon my child, enabling her to see visions and dream dreams.[2] Give my child the confidence and courage to run with the vision You give her.[3] Allow nothing to get in the way to sidetrack her. Help her to keep her eyes fixed on You.[4]

Thank You for Your promise to complete the work You have already begun in her life.[5] You have declared that the people who know their God shall be strong and do great exploits.[6] Help her to know and follow Your Word so she will be able to experience great success in all that she does.[7] In Jesus' name!

GOD'S WORD SAYS

1. "He who dwells in the shelter of the Most High will rest in the shadow of the Almighty" (Ps. 91:1).

2. "Then no harm will befall you, no disaster will come near your tent. For he will command his angels concerning you to guard you in all your ways" (Ps. 91:10-11).

3. "The angel of the Lord encamps around those who fear him, and he delivers them" (Ps. 34:7).

4. "Who through faith are shielded by God's power until the coming of the salvation that is ready to be revealed in the last time" (1 Pet. 1:5).

5. "Then you will go on your way in safety, and your foot will not stumble" (Prov. 3:23).

6. "You will keep in perfect peace him whose mind is steadfast, because he trusts in you" (Is. 26:3).

7. "A thousand may fall at your side, ten thousand at your right hand, but it will not come near you" (Ps. 91:7).

8. "'Because he loves me,' says the Lord, 'I will rescue him; I will protect him, for he acknowledges my name'" (Ps. 91:14).

7

DIVINE PROTECTION

Heavenly Father, in the name of Jesus thank You for being a refuge and fortress for my child. He dwells in Your shadow[1] so no evil shall befall him, no accident shall overtake him, and no plague shall come near our home. You command Your angels to his side, guarding him in all his ways.[2] Your angels encamp around him and deliver him in every circumstance.[3]

I release my faith in Your Word to protect _____ by the power of God.[4] You have promised that my child will go on his way in safety, and he will not so much as stumble.[5] You will keep him in perfect peace because his mind is stayed on You.[6] He can trust in Your shield of faithfulness! Even if a thousand were to fall at his side and ten thousand at his right hand, he will not have to fear because trouble will not come near him.[7] You rescue him and protect him simply because he loves You.[8] In Jesus' name, amen!

God's Word Says

1. "Give, and it will be given to you. A good measure, pressed down, shaken together and running over, will be poured into your lap. For with the measure you use, it will be measured to you" (Luke 6:38).

2. "The people are bringing more than enough for doing the work the Lord commanded to be done. Then Moses gave an order and they sent this word throughout the camp: 'No man or woman is to make anything else as an offering for the sanctuary.' And so the people were restrained from bringing more, because what they already had was more than enough to do all the work" (Ex. 36:5-7).

3. "Do not be deceived: God cannot be mocked. A man reaps what he sows. The one who sows to please his sinful nature, from that nature will reap destruction; the one who sows to please the Spirit, from the Spirit will reap eternal life" (Gal. 6:7-8).

4. "Each man should give what he has decided in his heart to give, not reluctantly or under compulsion, for God loves a cheerful giver" (2 Cor. 9:7).

5. "The proverbs of Solomon son of David, king of Israel: for attaining wisdom and discipline; for understanding words of insight; for acquiring a disciplined and prudent life, doing what is right and just and fair; for giving prudence to the simple, knowledge and discretion to the young — let the wise listen and add to their learning, and let the discerning get guidance" (Prov. 1:1-5).

6. "The Lord answered, 'Who then is the faithful and wise manager, whom the master puts in charge of his servants to give them their food allowance at the proper time?'" (Luke 12:42).

8
GIVING

Heavenly Father, thank You for the greatest gift of all — the gift of Your Son Jesus that we might have abundant life. Thank You for placing Your giving nature into my child when she was born-again. Allow that nature to shine forth in her life, and fulfill Your promise to give back to her, in good measure, pressed down, shaken together and running over.[1]

Father, teach _____ to give so freely that You will have more than enough to do Your work.[2] Thank You for causing the principles of sowing and reaping to be real to her,[3] enabling her to give in such a way that she will reap a mighty harvest. Help her to give cheerfully, for You love a cheerful giver.[4]

Father, I praise You for giving _____ supernatural wisdom in the area of finances.[5] May she be a good steward not only of her money but of everything You have entrusted to her.[6] In Jesus' name.

GOD'S WORD SAYS

1. "May he give you the desire of your heart and make all your plans succeed" (Ps. 20:4).

2. "Show me your ways, O Lord, teach me your paths" (Ps. 25:4).

3. "If my people, who are called by my name, will humble themselves and pray and seek my face and turn from their wicked ways, then will I hear from heaven and will forgive their sin and will heal their land" (2 Chr. 7:14).

4. "For you have delivered me from death and my feet from stumbling, that I may walk before God in the light of life" (Ps. 56:13).

   "Be at rest once more, O my soul, for the Lord has been good to you" (Ps. 116:7).

5. "For though a righteous man falls seven times, he rises again, but the wicked are brought down by calamity" (Prov. 24:16).

6. "And we know that in all things God works for the good of those who love him, who have been called according to his purpose" (Rom. 8:28).

7. "No, in all these things we are more than conquerors through him who loved us" (Rom. 8:37).

9
GOD'S WILL

Heavenly Father, show _____ Your direction and purpose for his life.[1] Show him Your ways and Your will for his life, teaching him to walk upon Your paths.[2] Cause him to walk humbly before You, to have a great desire to seek Your face and to turn from every path of wickedness.[3] The plans and purposes that You have for my child are great!

Keep my child on the right path. Keep his feet from stumbling.[4] Let him walk in Your perfect will, and let nothing trip him up. Even if he does fall down, thank You for the power You have given him to get back up again.[5] Father, You're working all things for his good no matter what comes his way.[6] Help him to walk in Your will confidently, recognizing that he is more than a conqueror with Your help.[7] In Jesus' name.

GOD'S WORD SAYS

1. "For he chose us in him before the creation of the world to be holy and blameless in his sight. In love he predestined us to be adopted as his sons through Jesus Christ, in accordance with his pleasure and will — to the praise of his glorious grace, which he has freely given us in the One he loves" (Eph. 1:4-6).

2. "For you are a people holy to the Lord your God. The Lord your God has chosen you out of all the peoples on the face of the earth to be his people, his treasured possession" (Deut. 7:6).

3. "I in them and you in me. May they be brought to complete unity to let the world know that you sent me and have loved them even as you have loved me" (John 17:23).

4. "For his anger lasts only a moment, but his favor lasts a lifetime; weeping may remain for a night, but rejoicing comes in the morning" (Ps. 30:5).

5. "But he said to me, 'My grace is sufficient for you, for my power is made perfect in weakness.' Therefore I will boast all the more gladly about my weaknesses, so that Christ's power may rest on me" (2 Cor. 12:9).

6. "May our Lord Jesus Christ himself and God our Father, who loved us and by his grace gave us eternal encouragement and good hope, encourage your hearts and strengthen you in every good deed and word" (2 Thess. 2:16-17).

10

GRACE AND FAVOR

Father, thank You for choosing _____ even before You created the world, for adopting her as Your own daughter and transforming her to be holy and blameless through Your glorious grace.[1] She belongs to You and has become a treasured possession in Your sight.[2] Thank You for loving her with the same love You have for Jesus.[3] Thank You for Your favor that You have given her, which will last throughout her lifetime![4]

Father, I am so grateful for Your unmerited favor and grace. And I thank You, Lord, that Your grace is sufficient for my child.[5] Help her to comprehend the truth that at her weakest and most vulnerable moments, Your grace and power will be made perfect.

Help _____ to live with a constant awareness of Your love and grace that gives her eternal encouragement and good hope, and strengthens her for every good deed and word.[6] In Jesus' name.

GOD'S WORD SAYS

1. "Train a child in the way he should go, and when he is old he will not turn from it" (Prov. 22:6).

2. "Those who are led by the Spirit of God are sons of God" (Rom. 8:14).

3. "The integrity of the upright guides them, but the unfaithful are destroyed by their duplicity" (Prov. 11:3).

4. "I will lead the blind by ways they have not known, along unfamiliar paths I will guide them; I will turn the darkness into light before them and make the rough places smooth. These are the things I will do; I will not forsake them" (Is. 42:16).

5. "Since you are my rock and my fortress, for the sake of your name lead and guide me" (Ps. 31:3).

6. "I will instruct you and teach you in the way you should go; I will counsel you and watch over you" (Ps. 32:8).

7. "You guide me with your counsel, and afterward you will take me into glory" (Ps. 73:24).

8. "Wilt thou not from this time cry unto me, My father, thou art the guide of my youth?" (Jer. 3:4, KJV).

9. "Do not conform any longer to the pattern of this world, but be transformed by the renewing of your mind. Then you will be able to test and approve what God's will is — his good, pleasing and perfect will" (Rom. 12:2).

10. "The Lord will guide you always; he will satisfy your needs in a sun-scorched land and will strengthen your frame. You will be like a well-watered garden, like a spring whose waters never fail" (Is. 58:11).

11
GUIDANCE

Heavenly Father, thank You that _____ is born-again and serving You. Your Word says that if he is trained up in the way he should go, when he is old he will not depart from it.[1] Thank You for leading him by Your Spirit.[2] You said that my child's integrity will guide him,[3] and so I am asking You to lead him with guidance that only comes from Your Spirit. You are a guide to the blind and a light to those who cannot see.[4] You are his rock and fortress to lead and guide him.[5]

Thank You for instructing my son in the way he should go and for watching over him.[6] Guide him with Your counsel.[7]

Lord, *You* are the guide of our youth,[8] not the media, not their friends but You! I give You praise for renewing my child's mind according to Your Word. Show him what Your good and perfect will is for him.[9] Thank You, Lord, for continual divine direction that leads to the best You have for him.[10] My child is in Your hands, and for that I am grateful.

GOD'S WORD SAYS

1. "And afterward, I will pour out my Spirit on all people. Your sons and daughters will prophesy, your old men will dream dreams, your young men will see visions" (Joel 2:28).

2. "Blessed are those who hunger and thirst for righteousness, for they will be filled" (Matt. 5:6).

3. "As the deer pants for streams of water, so my soul pants for you, O God" (Ps. 42:1).

4. "Come near to God and he will come near to you. Wash your hands, you sinners, and purify your hearts, you double-minded" (James 4:8).

5. "Submit yourselves, then, to God. Resist the devil, and he will flee from you" (James 4:7).

6. "Finally, brethren, pray for us, that the word of the Lord may have free course, and be glorified, even as it is with you" (2 Thess. 3:1, KJV).

12
HUNGERING FOR GOD

Dear heavenly Father, thank You for the opportunity
to train up _____ with Your Word. I praise You for my
child's love for You. I remind You that Your Word says You
will pour out Your Spirit in the last days, and our sons and
daughters will prophesy.[1] So right now I'm asking You to
pour out Your Spirit on my daughter. Give her a hunger for
You such as she has never had before — a hunger for righteousness, a hunger for Your Word and a hunger to spend
time in Your presence. You promised to fill those who
hunger and thirst after righteousness.[2]

As a deer longs to get a drink, so let my child
thirst for You.[3] As she draws
near to You, You will
draw near to her.[4] Right
now in Jesus' name, I
take authority over any
opposition that would try to hin-
der the work You want to do in my child's life.[5] I release
Your Word and Your Spirit to have free course in her life.[6]

GOD'S WORD SAYS

1. "This is the day the Lord has made; let us rejoice and be glad in it" (Ps. 118:24).

2. "Rejoice in the Lord always. I will say it again: Rejoice!" (Phil. 4:4).

3. "Though you have not seen him, you love him; and even though you do not see him now, you believe in him and are filled with an inexpressible and glorious joy" (1 Pet. 1:8).

4. "Nehemiah said, 'Go and enjoy choice food and sweet drinks, and send some to those who have nothing prepared. This day is sacred to our Lord. Do not grieve, for the joy of the Lord is your strength'" (Neh. 8:10).

5. "If you falter in times of trouble, how small is your strength!" (Prov. 24:10).

6. "All the days of the oppressed are wretched, but the cheerful heart has a continual feast" (Prov. 15:15).

7. "And provide for those who grieve in Zion — to bestow on them a crown of beauty instead of ashes, the oil of gladness instead of mourning, and a garment of praise instead of a spirit of despair. They will be called oaks of righteousness, a planting of the Lord for the display of his splendor" (Is. 61:3).

8. "We write this to make our joy complete" (1 John 1:4).

9. "I have told you this so that my joy may be in you and that your joy may be complete" (John 15:11).

10. "You have made known to me the paths of life; you will fill me with joy in your presence" (Acts 2:28).

13
JOY

Heavenly Father, thank You for giving us a brand-new day; a day to rejoice in You![1] Flood _____ with Your joy, causing a continual gladness in his heart![2] Thank You, Jesus, for giving us so much of Your joy that words cannot describe it.[3]

Allow Your joy to energize and strengthen him today.[4] Give him the strength to withstand every adversity that may come his way.[5] Let his heart have a continual celebration because of what You have done for him.[6]

I declare victory over the spirit of heaviness in his life and ask You to replace it with the garment of praise![7] I thank You, God, that the devil cannot steal my child's joy. Allow Your Word to burn in his heart, producing a fullness of joy that comes only from You![8] Such joy will remain with him throughout his life[9] and will affect others. I pray people will see Jesus in his countenance.[10] In Jesus' name!

GOD'S WORD SAYS

1. "Before they call I will answer; while they are still speaking I will hear" (Is. 65:24).

2. "You know the message God sent to the people of Israel, telling the good news of peace through Jesus Christ, who is Lord of all" (Acts 10:36).

3. "How can a young man keep his way pure? By living according to your word" (Ps.119:9).

4. "Immediately, something like scales fell from Saul's eyes, and he could see again. He got up and was baptized" (Acts 9:18).

5. "You may ask me for anything in my name, and I will do it" (John 14:14).

6. "And after the earthquake a fire; but the Lord was not in the fire: and after the fire a still small voice" (1 Kin. 19:12, KJV).

7. "You hear, O Lord, the desire of the afflicted; you encourage them, and you listen to their cry" (Ps. 10:17).

8. "I will give them an undivided heart and put a new spirit in them; I will remove from them their heart of stone and give them a heart of flesh" (Ezek. 11:19).

   "I will give you a new heart and put a new spirit in you; I will remove from you your heart of stone and give you a heart of flesh" (Ezek. 36:26).

9. "Because of the increase of wickedness, the love of most will grow cold" (Matt. 24:12).

14

THE LORDSHIP OF CHRIST

Heavenly Father, I cry out to You right now in the name of Jesus for _____, knowing You will answer me.[1] You know my child's heart, and You desire to be the Lord of all her life.[2] Cause her heart to be receptive to Your Spirit and Your Word.[3] Thank You for taking the blinders off her eyes[4] and revealing Yourself to her.

Because Your Word says that we can receive whatever we ask in Your name,[5] I'm asking You in the name of Your Son, Jesus, to fill _____ with Your presence.

Allow my child to hear You as You speak to her with Your still small voice.[6] Give her an ear to hear.[7] May her heart never become calloused,[8] and may her love for You never turn cold.[9] Thank You, Jesus, for being the Lord over every area of _____'s life. You are not just her Savior — but her Lord!

God's Word Says

1. "Love never fails" (1 Cor. 13:8).

2. "For God so loved the world that he gave his one and only Son, that whoever believes in him shall not perish but have eternal life" (John 3:16).

3. "A new command I give you: Love one another. As I have loved you, so you must love one another" (John 13:34-35).

4. "And hope does not disappoint us, because God has poured out his love into our hearts by the Holy Spirit, whom he has given us" (Rom. 5:5).

5. "This is love: not that we loved God, but that he loved us and sent his Son as an atoning sacrifice for our sins" (1 John 4:10).

6. "And so we know and rely on the love God has for us. God is love. Whoever lives in love lives in God" (1 John 4:16).

7. "Love is patient, love is kind. It does not envy, it does not boast, it is not proud. It is not rude, it is not self-seeking, it is not easily angered, it keeps no record of wrongs. Love does not delight in evil but rejoices with the truth. It always protects, always trusts, always hopes, always perseveres" (1 Cor. 13:4-7).

15

LOVE

Dear heavenly Father, thank You for Your unfailing love.[1] Thank You for sending Your Son, Jesus, to shed His blood for us.[2] Thank You, Jesus, for being obedient unto death so we could have life. I love You, Jesus, and lift up my child to You right now. Fill him with Your love until it radiates from his very being. Then others will know he belongs to You.[3] You have poured Your supernatural love into his heart by the Holy Spirit.[4]

Give _____ a better understanding of Your love. Show him what real love is.[5] Let him sense Your presence, and cause him to see how much You love him.[6] Thank You, Jesus, for causing him to love others the way You love him.[7]

GOD'S WORD SAYS

1. "Diligent hands will rule, but laziness ends in slave labor" (Prov. 12:24).

2. "Lazy hands make a man poor, but diligent hands bring wealth" (Prov. 10:4).

3. "Do you see a man skilled in his work? He will serve before kings; he will not serve before obscure men" (Prov. 22:29).

4. "Submit yourselves, then, to God. Resist the devil, and he will flee from you" (James 4:7).

5. "We do not want you to become lazy, but to imitate those who through faith and patience inherit what has been promised" (Heb. 6:12).

6. "For it is God who works in you to will and to act according to his good purpose" (Phil. 2:13).

7. "There is surely a future hope for you, and your hope will not be cut off" (Prov. 23:18).

16
MOTIVATION

Heavenly Father, fill my child with a motivation to live for You. Cause her to be diligent in all that she does.[1] Thank You for Your Word which teaches her that diligence produces rewards.[2] You will cause her to stand before important men because of her faithful, competent work record.[3]

Right now in Jesus name I rebuke laziness, apathy and complacency from her life! I refuse to allow them to have a hold upon my child.[4]

Thank You for giving _____ faith and patience to fulfill what You have called her to do.[5] Work in my child to will and act according to Your purpose.[6] Your purpose will give her the hope of a blessed future.[7] In Jesus' name!

GOD'S WORD SAYS

1. "And in the church God has appointed first of all apostles, second prophets, third teachers, then workers of miracles, also those having gifts of healing, those able to help others, those with gifts of administration, and those speaking in different kinds of tongues" (1 Cor. 12:28).

2. "The fear of the Lord is the beginning of knowledge, but fools despise wisdom and discipline" (Prov. 1:7).

3. "Blessed are those servants, whom the lord when he cometh shall find watching: verily I say unto you, that he shall gird himself, and make them to sit down to meat, and will come forth and serve them" (Luke 12:37, KJV).

4. "For surely, O Lord, you bless the righteous; you surround them with your favor as with a shield" (Ps. 5:12).

5. "And the Lord answered me, and said, Write the vision, and make it plain upon tables, that he may run that readeth it" (Hab. 2:2, KJV).

6. "Listen, my son, accept what I say, and the years of your life will be many" (Prov. 4:10).

17
PASTORAL RELATIONSHIPS

Heavenly Father, thank You for sending Pastor _____ into my child's life. I pray that my child will mature in You under his leadership, for You have appointed leaders over us to train and teach us.[1] Cause him to remain teachable, because Your Word says that only fools refuse to be taught.[2] Give _____ respect for his leaders so he can be a blessing to the entire church.

Thank You for putting a servant's heart within him, for You have pronounced a blessing on the servants of the Lord.[3] I ask You to continue to surround him with a shield of favor[4] and to extend that favor to his pastor and the relationship they share. Thank You for our pastor's vision, and empower my child to run with that vision.[5]

Father, I ask You to continue to give my child a willingness to receive leadership, causing the years of his life to be many as he receives Your sayings.[6] Thank You, Father, for allowing my son to be a blessing to the church and kingdom of God!

God's Word Says

1. "For God is greater than our hearts, and he knows everything" (1 John 3:20).

2. "And the peace of God, which transcends all understanding, will guard your hearts and your minds in Christ Jesus" (Phil. 4:7).

3. "May the God of hope fill you with all joy and peace as you trust in him, so that you may overflow with hope by the power of the Holy Spirit" (Rom. 15:13).

4. "It teaches us to say 'No' to ungodliness and worldly passions, and to live self-controlled, upright and godly lives in this present age" (Titus 2:12).

5. "'For who has known the mind of the Lord that he may instruct him?' But we have the mind of Christ" (1 Cor. 2:16).

6. "You will keep in perfect peace him whose mind is steadfast, because he trusts in you" (Is. 26:3).

7. "And we know that in all things God works for the good of those who love him, who have been called according to his purpose" (Rom. 8:28).

18
PEACE

Heavenly Father, You know every circumstance that my child goes through and every trial she encounters.[1] Fill _____ with Your peace — peace of God which passes all understanding. Thank You, Lord, not only for filling my child with Your peace but for guarding her heart with that peace.[2] Your promise of joy and peace will cause her to abound in hope through the power of the Holy Spirit![3]

Father, equip her with the power to say no to ungodliness and things that are not of You![4] I declare right now in Jesus' name that _____ has the mind of Christ![5] Keep her in perfect peace because her mind is stayed on You.[6]

Thank You, Father, for working all things together for good no matter what situations my child may encounter.[7] In Jesus' name.

GOD'S WORD SAYS

1. "I love those who love me, and those who seek me find me" (Prov. 8:17).

2. "For the word of God is living and active. Sharper than any double-edged sword, it penetrates even to dividing soul and spirit, joints and marrow; it judges the thoughts and attitudes of the heart" (Heb. 4:12).

3. "Holding forth the word of life; that I may rejoice in the day of Christ, that I have not run in vain, neither laboured in vain" (Phil. 2:16, KJV).

4. "All Scripture is God-breathed and is useful for teaching, rebuking, correcting and training in righteousness" (2 Tim. 3:16).

5. "Your word is a lamp to my feet and a light for my path" (Ps. 119:105).

6. "I have hidden your word in my heart that I might not sin against you" (Ps. 119:11).

7. "Do not be anxious about anything, but in everything, by prayer and petition, with thanksgiving, present your requests to God" (Phil. 4:6).

8. "I love you, O Lord, my strength. The Lord is my rock, my fortress and my deliverer; my God is my rock, in whom I take refuge. He is my shield and the horn of my salvation, my stronghold" (Ps. 18:1-2).

9. "For you have been my refuge, a strong tower against the foe" (Ps. 61:3).

19
PERSONAL DEVOTIONS

Heavenly Father, continue to increase my child's love for You. Do a work in his devotional life. Give him a supernatural hunger for the Word of God.[1] Empower Your Word to come alive in my son, for Your Word is living and active, and there's unlimited power in it![2] Cause Your Word to jump off the pages into my child's innermost being.[3] Speak to him through Your Word and Spirit,[4] and let his mind and heart be alert to what You have to say. For Your Word keeps us from sin[5] and is like a light that helps us see Your way.[6]

I pray also, Lord, that _____ will spend time just talking and fellowshipping with You. You said to be anxious about nothing but in everything come to You in prayer.[7] Thank You for dropping the desire into my child's heart to spend time with You. You are a fort into which we can enter and be safe; You are a mountain in which we can hide.[8] You are a tower of safety.[9] Thank You that my son is drawing closer to You and is in Your hands.

God's Word Says

1. "Be joyful in hope, patient in affliction, faithful in prayer" (Rom. 12:12).

2. "Repent, then, and turn to God, so that your sins may be wiped out, that times of refreshing may come from the Lord" (Acts 3:19).

3. "Therefore confess your sins to each other and pray for each other so that you may be healed. The prayer of a righteous man is powerful and effective" (James 5:16).

4. "You may ask me for anything in my name, and I will do it" (John 14:14).

5. "Cast all your anxiety on him because he cares for you" (1 Pet. 5:7).

6. "The Lord is far from the wicked but he hears the prayer of the righteous" (Prov. 15:29).

7. "Now to him who is able to do immeasurably more than all we ask or imagine, according to his power that is at work within us" (Eph. 3:20).

8. "And we know that in all things God works for the good of those who love him, who have been called according to his purpose" (Rom. 8:28).

20
PRAYER LIFE

Heavenly Father, increase my child's desire to fellowship with You. Become so real to her that she will be aware of Your presence in her life, desiring to fellowship with You throughout the day and to be instant in prayer.[1] Let her time with You become her number one priority. I ask that she will discover the time she spends with You is refreshing to her spirit.[2]

Your Word declares that the effectual fervent prayer of a righteous man (or woman) is powerful and effective.[3] When we ask anything in Your name, You will do it[4] because You lovingly care for us.[5] I ask in faith that _____ will come to You in prayer freely about anything, knowing that You will listen and respond to her.[6] As she prays and believes, let her see Your power in operation to change the circumstances around her — exceedingly abundantly above all she can ask or think.[7] Work all things together for her good.[8] In Jesus' name.

God's Word Says

1. "For to us a child is born, to us a son is given, and the government will be on his shoulders. And he will be called Wonderful Counselor, Mighty God, Everlasting Father, Prince of Peace" (Is. 9:6).

2. "And the peace of God, which transcends all understanding, will guard your hearts and your minds in Christ Jesus" (Phil. 4:7).

3. "And take the helmet of salvation, and the sword of the Spirit, which is the word of God" (Eph. 6:17).

4. "We demolish arguments and every pretension that sets itself up against the knowledge of God, and we take captive every thought to make it obedient to Christ" (2 Cor. 10:5).

5. "To be made new in the attitude of your minds" (Eph. 4:23).

6. "Finally, brothers, whatever is true, whatever is noble, whatever is right, whatever is pure, whatever is lovely, whatever is admirable — if anything is excellent or praiseworthy — think about such things" (Phil. 4:8).

7. "Jesus replied: 'Love the Lord your God with all your heart and with all your soul and with all your mind'" (Matt. 22:37).

8. "For God did not give us a spirit of timidity, but a spirit of power, of love and of self-discipline" (2 Tim. 1:7).

21

Renewing of the Mind

Heavenly Father, I praise You that Jesus is the Prince of Peace[1] and because of that Your peace will keep my son's heart and mind in Christ Jesus.[2] Thank You for the helmet of salvation that guards _____ 's mind.[3] I pray that You will remove his old ways of thinking and any thoughts that aren't pleasing to You. Help him bring every thought captive to the obedience of Christ.[4] May Your Word renew every part of his attitude[5] so he will think on things that are true, noble, right, pure, lovely, excellent and praiseworthy![6]

Father, stir his heart to love You with all of his soul, all of his strength and all of his mind.[7] I thank You because Your Spirit is moving on my son causing his mind to be sound and his thoughts to be pure with Your blessing resting on every part of his life.[8] In Jesus' name!

GOD'S WORD SAYS

1. "God is our refuge and strength, an ever-present help in trouble" (Ps. 46:1).

2. "The Lord is my rock, my fortress and my deliverer; my God is my rock, in whom I take refuge. He is my shield and the horn of my salvation, my stronghold" (Ps. 18:2).

3. "You will have plenty to eat, until you are full, and you will praise the name of the Lord your God, who has worked wonders for you; never again will my people be shamed" (Joel 2:26).

4. "No temptation has seized you except what is common to man. And God is faithful; he will not let you be tempted beyond what you can bear. But when you are tempted, he will also provide a way out so that you can stand up under it" (1 Cor. 10:13).

5. "So if the Son sets you free, you will be free indeed" (John 8:36).

6. "Through Christ Jesus the law of the Spirit of life set me free from the law of sin and death" (Rom. 8:2).

7. "Submit yourselves, then, to God. Resist the devil, and he will flee from you" (James 4:7).

8. "Teaching us that, denying ungodliness and worldly lusts, we should live soberly, righteously, and godly, in this present world" (Titus 2:12).

22

RESISTING TEMPTATION

Heavenly Father, I praise You for Your goodness. You are our refuge and strength, an ever-present help in times of trouble![1] You are our deliverer, our fortress and our rock.[2] I put my whole trust in You and will never be put to shame.[3] Thank You that in any temptation You're the one who provides a way of escape.[4] You are bringing true freedom to my child.[5] I give You praise right now that my child is free from temptation and sin. Thank You, Jesus, for giving her power over sin and death.[6]

Father, You have promised that if we resist the devil, he will flee.[7] Thank You for giving _____ the strength to resist temptation. For Your Word teaches us to say no to ungodliness and worldly passions and to live self-controlled, upright and godly lives in this present age.[8] Thank You, Lord, for giving my child complete and total victory!

God's Word Says

1. "For he says, 'In the time of my favor I heard you, and in the day of salvation I helped you.' I tell you, now is the time of God's favor, now is the day of salvation" (2 Cor. 6:2).

2. "They replied, 'Believe in the Lord Jesus, and you will be saved — you and your household'" (Acts 16:31).

3. "Therefore I tell you, whatever you ask for in prayer, believe that you have received it, and it will be yours" (Mark 11:24).

4. "And it shall come to pass in that day, that his burden shall be taken away from off thy shoulder, and his yoke from off thy neck, and the yoke shall be destroyed because of the anointing" (Is. 10:27).

5. "The god of this age has blinded the minds of unbelievers, so that they cannot see the light of the gospel of the glory of Christ, who is the image of God" (2 Cor. 4:4).

6. "The eyes of your understanding being enlightened; that you may know what is the hope of His calling, what are the riches of the glory of His inheritance in the saints" (Eph. 1:18, NKJV).

7. "He who has an ear, let him hear what the Spirit says to the churches" (Rev. 2:29).

8. "Or do you show contempt for the riches of his kindness, tolerance and patience, not realizing that God's kindness leads you toward repentance?" (Rom. 2:4).

9. "Ask the Lord of the harvest, therefore, to send out workers into his harvest field" (Matt. 9:38).

10. "Are not all angels ministering spirits sent to serve those who will inherit salvation?" (Heb. 1:14).

11. "You yourselves are our letter, written on our hearts, known and read by everybody" (2 Cor. 3:2).

23
SALVATION

Heavenly Father, thank You that today is the day of salvation.[1] I know that You love my family and that Your Spirit is working on them to be saved.[2] Therefore, thank You for moving on _____, and I praise You for his salvation right now.[3]

I release Your anointing to break every hindrance that would try to prevent him from receiving Jesus as his Savior.[4] I come against every obstruction that has distorted the truth of the gospel.[5] Thank You that the eyes of his understanding are being unveiled,[6] and his ears are being opened to Your Word.[7] As You reveal Your goodness to him, You will lead him to repentance.[8]

Father, send forth laborers this day to minister Your Word to him.[9] I give You praise for Your angels who are also ministering to him throughout this day, drawing him home to Jesus, for he is an heir of salvation.[10]

Help me to be the example You have called me to be for my child so that he will see Jesus alive in my life.[11]

GOD'S WORD SAYS

1. "The wicked man flees though no one pursues, but the righteous are as bold as a lion" (Prov. 28:1).

2. "After they prayed, the place where they were meeting was shaken. And they were all filled with the Holy Spirit and spoke the word of God boldly" (Acts 4:31).

3. "For God did not give us a spirit of timidity, but a spirit of power, of love and of self-discipline" (2 Tim. 1:7).

4. "So do not be ashamed to testify about our Lord, or ashamed of me his prisoner. But join with me in suffering for the gospel, by the power of God" (2 Tim. 1:8).

5. "I am not ashamed of the gospel, because it is the power of God for the salvation of everyone who believes: first for the Jew, then for the Gentile" (Rom. 1:16).

6. "A great door for effective work has opened to me, and there are many who oppose me" (1 Cor. 16:9).

7. "I can do everything through him who gives me strength" (Phil. 4:13).

8. "But you will receive power when the Holy Spirit comes on you; and you will be my witnesses in Jerusalem, and in all Judea and Samaria, and to the ends of the earth" (Acts 1:8).

9. "After they prayed, the place where they were meeting was shaken. And they were all filled with the Holy Spirit and spoke the word of God boldly" (Acts 4:31).

10. "For surely, O Lord, you bless the righteous; you surround them with your favor as with a shield" (Ps. 5:12).

11. "He said to them, 'Go into all the world and preach the good news to all creation'" (Mark 16:15).

24
SHARING JESUS

Dear heavenly Father, thank You for my child and the anointing on her life. I pray You give _____ a new boldness which she has never before experienced.[1] This boldness will help her to effectively share her faith.[2] You have not given her a spirit of fear but of power, love and a sound mind,[3] so she does not need to be ashamed to testify about You.[4] Thank You, Father, that she is not ashamed of the gospel of Christ.[5]

Give her effective opportunities to share her faith[6] and the strength to share You with others,[7] to be a witness to everyone she meets.[8]

Thank You, Lord, that she is walking in Your boldness today — Holy Ghost boldness.[9] You are giving her favor with everyone she comes into contact with.[10] You are using her to spark revival in her school and to touch everyone around her. This is the day![11]

GOD'S WORD SAYS

1. "Give, and it will be given to you. A good measure, pressed down, shaken together and running over, will be poured into your lap. For with the measure you use, it will be measured to you" (Luke 6:38).

2. "All these are the work of one and the same Spirit, and he gives them to each one, just as he determines" (1 Cor. 12:11).

3. "But seek first his kingdom and his righteousness, and all these things will be given to you as well" (Matt. 6:33).

4. "Follow the way of love and eagerly desire spiritual gifts, especially the gift of prophecy" (1 Cor. 14:1).

5. "So it is with you. Since you are eager to have spiritual gifts, try to excel in gifts that build up the church" (1 Cor. 14:12).

6. "But eagerly desire the greater gifts. And now I will show you the most excellent way" (1 Cor. 12:31).

7. "Do your best to present yourself to God as one approved, a workman who does not need to be ashamed and who correctly handles the word of truth" (2 Tim. 2:15).

8. "To one there is given through the Spirit the message of wisdom, to another the message of knowledge by means of the same Spirit, to another faith by the same Spirit, to another gifts of healing by that one Spirit, to another miraculous powers, to another prophecy, to another distinguishing between spirits, to another speaking in different kinds of tongues, and to still another the interpretation of tongues" (1 Cor. 12:8-10).

9. "And afterward, I will pour out my Spirit on all people. Your sons and daughters will prophesy, your old men will dream dreams, your young men will see visions" (Joel 2:28).

25
SPIRITUAL GIFTS

Heavenly Father, I come before You today to praise You for who You are. Thank You, Lord, that You are a giver.[1] You desire to give spiritual gifts[2] not just to me but to my children. Father, as we seek You first You will add blessings to our lives.[3] Cause _____ to desire spiritual gifts[4] as well as to excel in them.[5]

Thank You, Lord, that my child will covet these[6] spiritual gifts and study them.[7] Burn in his heart a desire to move in Your gifts to bless the body of Christ with the word of wisdom, the word of knowledge, gift of faith, gifts of healings, working of miracles, discerning of spirits, tongues and the interpretation of tongues.[8] You said that in the last days You will pour out Your Spirit on all flesh. You said our sons and daughters will prophesy.[9] Thank You, Jesus, for pouring out Your Spirit on my child. He will never be the same!

God's Word Says

1. "But you, dear friends, build yourselves up in your most holy faith and pray in the Holy Spirit" (Jude 20).

2. "Therefore, my dear brothers, stand firm. Let nothing move you. Always give yourselves fully to the work of the Lord, because you know that your labor in the Lord is not in vain" (1 Cor. 15:58).

3. "He says to himself, 'Nothing will shake me; I'll always be happy and never have trouble'" (Ps. 10:6).

4. "If thou faint in the day of adversity, thy strength is small" (Prov. 24:10).

5. "Finally, be strong in the Lord and in his mighty power. Put on the full armor of God so that you can take your stand against the devil's schemes. Therefore put on the full armor of God, so that when the day of evil comes, you may be able to stand your ground, and after you have done everything, to stand" (Eph. 6:10-11,13).

6. "Therefore, my dear brothers, stand firm. Let nothing move you. Always give yourselves fully to the work of the Lord, because you know that your labor in the Lord is not in vain" (1 Cor. 15:58).

7. "We have come to share in Christ if we hold firmly till the end the confidence we had at first" (Heb. 3:14).

8. "The Lord will make you the head, not the tail. If you pay attention to the commands of the Lord your God that I give you this day and carefully follow them, you will always be at the top, never at the bottom...He will lend to you, but you will not lend to him. He will be the head, but you will be the tail" (Deut. 28:13,44).

9. "No, in all these things we are more than conquerors through him who loved us" (Rom. 8:37).

26

STEADFASTNESS

Heavenly Father, thank You for my child's life. Thank You for causing her to serve You with her whole heart. Father, You said in Your Word to build ourselves up by our most holy faith.[1] Thank You for causing my children to build themselves up in Your Word to the point that they will not waver. This day I give You praise because _____ will not stray but is steadfast and immovable![2] Even in the midst of adversity, she will not be moved.[3] Your Word says that if we faint in the day of adversity, our strength is small.[4] But my child's strength is not small — she is strong in You!

Thank You for the full armor of God which equips her to stand firm.[5] Nothing will be able to move her, for she knows that her labor is not in vain.[6] Give her a holy determination to serve You.

Thank You, Jesus, that she will stand steadfast until the very end.[7] She is the head and not the tail.[8] She is going over and not under. She is more than a conqueror![9] Victory belongs to her!

GOD'S WORD SAYS

1. "And these signs will accompany those who believe: In my name they will drive out demons; they will speak in new tongues" (Mark 16:17).

2. "When Paul placed his hands on them, the Holy Spirit came on them, and they spoke in tongues and prophesied" (Acts 19:6).

3. "So what shall I do? I will pray with my spirit, but I will also pray with my mind; I will sing with my spirit, but I will also sing with my mind" (1 Cor. 14:15).

4. "They saw what seemed to be tongues of fire that separated and came to rest on each of them" (Acts 2:3).

5. "In the same way, the Spirit helps us in our weakness. We do not know what we ought to pray for, but the Spirit himself intercedes for us with groans that words cannot express" (Rom. 8:26).

6. "But you will receive power when the Holy Spirit comes on you; and you will be my witnesses in Jerusalem, and in all Judea and Samaria, and to the ends of the earth" (Acts 1:8).

27
TONGUES

Heavenly Father, thank You for the power of the Holy Spirit and the ability to speak in tongues. Father, I lift up my child to You today. Thank for his life. Thank You for baptizing him in Your Holy Ghost. You said in Your Word that signs will follow those who believe. In Your name we will speak with new tongues.[1] When Paul laid hands on the people, the Holy Ghost fell on them, and they began to speak with other tongues.[2] Your Word also says that we all should speak in tongues.[3] This includes _____. Just as cloven tongues of fire fell on those in the upper room,[4] so let the fire of Your Holy Ghost fall on him! I pray that he will exercise the gift of tongues in his life.

Thank You for this powerful tool that will help him to pray even when he doesn't know what to pray. Your Holy Spirit is there to assist him.[5] Let the gift of tongues bubble out of him like a river. Fill him to overflowing. Thank You, Jesus, for filling my child with Your equipping power![6]

God's Word Says

1. "For this reason, since the day we heard about you, we have not stopped praying for you and asking God to fill you with the knowledge of his will through all spiritual wisdom and understanding" (Col. 1:9).

2. "The fear of the Lord is the beginning of wisdom; all who follow his precepts have good understanding. To him belongs eternal praise" (Ps. 111:10).

3. "Your word is a lamp to my feet and a light for my path" (Ps. 119:105).

4. "The entrance of your words gives light; it gives understanding to the simple" (Ps. 119:130).

5. "I pray also that the eyes of your heart may be enlightened in order that you may know the hope to which he has called you, the riches of his glorious inheritance in the saints" (Eph. 1:18).

6. "Do your best to present yourself to God as one approved, a workman who does not need to be ashamed and who correctly handles the word of truth" (2 Tim. 2:15).

7. "For the word of God is living and active. Sharper than any double-edged sword, it penetrates even to dividing soul and spirit, joints and marrow; it judges the thoughts and attitudes of the heart" (Heb. 4:12).

8. "Understanding is a fountain of life to those who have it, but folly brings punishment to fools" (Prov. 16:22).

28

UNDERSTANDING THE BIBLE

Heavenly Father, You are the God of wisdom and understanding, and I want to thank You for making understanding available to _____.[1] You said those who do Your commandments will have supernatural understanding.[2] My child needs Your understanding; she needs to understand Your Word. It is a lamp unto her feet and a light unto her path.[3] It gives light and understanding to the simple.[4]

Without the Word we cannot see where we're going. Father, open the eyes of my child's understanding so that she will see and understand Your mysteries.[5] Cause her mind to be alert and her heart to be receptive to what Your Word says. I pray that she will study to show herself approved unto You.[6] Make Your Word come alive in her heart today.[7] Let the words jump off the pages and breathe life into my child! Thank You for giving her revelation and understanding of Your Word, for it shall be a wellspring of life to her.[8]

God's Word Says

1. "For it is God who works in you to will and to act according to his good purpose" (Phil. 2:13).

2. "May the words of my mouth and the meditation of my heart be pleasing in your sight, O Lord, my Rock and my Redeemer" (Ps. 19:14).

3. "Therefore each of you must put off falsehood and speak truthfully to his neighbor, for we are all members of one body" (Eph. 4:25).

4. "The mouth of the righteous man utters wisdom, and his tongue speaks what is just" (Ps. 37:30).

5. "They will tell of the glory of your kingdom and speak of your might" (Ps. 145:11).

6. "I will extol the Lord at all times; his praise will always be on my lips" (Ps. 34:1).

7. "My dear brothers, take note of this: Everyone should be quick to listen, slow to speak and slow to become angry" (James 1:19).

8. "Set a guard over my mouth, O Lord; keep watch over the door of my lips" (Ps. 141:3).

9. "He who guards his mouth and his tongue keeps himself from calamity" (Prov. 21:23).

10. "Whoever would love life and see good days must keep his tongue from evil and his lips from deceitful speech" (1 Pet. 3:10).

11. "My soul will be satisfied as with the richest of foods; with singing lips my mouth will praise you" (Ps. 63:5).

29
WORDS OF THE MOUTH

Dear heavenly Father, I come before You today on behalf of _____. Thank You for the work that You are doing in his life.[1] You said to let the words of our mouths be acceptable in Your sight.[2] I release Your anointing in his life to cause his words to be acceptable in Your sight. May only good, edifying words come forth from his mouth.[3] You said in Your Word that the mouth of the righteous speak wisdom.[4] Let his mouth speak the praises of God.[5] David said Your praise would continually be on his mouth.[6] Let Your praises also be continually in my child's mouth.

I pray he will be quick to listen, slow to speak and slow to wrath[7] because there is power in our words. Thank You, Lord, that You have set a guard on his mouth.[8] Help him to watch his words and avoid trouble.[9] He will love life and see good days because he keeps his tongue from evil.[10]

Right now, Lord, I declare that my child's mouth will praise You with joyful lips![11]

SECTION II

BONDAGE-BREAKING PRAYERS

God's Word Says

1. "He heals the brokenhearted and binds up their wounds" (Ps. 147:3).

2. "If we confess our sins, he is faithful and just and will forgive us our sins and purify us from all unrighteousness" (1 John 1:9).

3. "Create in me a pure heart, O God, and renew a steadfast spirit within me. Do not cast me from your presence or take your Holy Spirit from me. Restore to me the joy of your salvation and grant me a willing spirit, to sustain me" (Ps. 51:10-12).

4. "And the peace of God, which transcends all understanding, will guard your hearts and your minds in Christ Jesus" (Phil. 4:7).

5. "Forget the former things; do not dwell on the past. See, I am doing a new thing! Now it springs up; do you not perceive it? I am making a way in the desert and streams in the wasteland" (Is. 43:18-19).

6. "Brothers, I do not consider myself yet to have taken hold of it. But one thing I do: Forgetting what is behind and straining toward what is ahead, I press on toward the goal to win the prize for which God has called me heavenward in Christ Jesus" (Phil. 3:13-14).

7. "I led them with cords of human kindness, with ties of love; I lifted the yoke from their neck and bent down to feed them" (Hos. 11:4).

30
ABORTION (ALREADY HAD ONE)

Dear heavenly Father, I lift up my daughter to You. You said in Your Word that You heal the brokenhearted.[1] Please heal her heart. Wrap Your arms around her with Your love. Thank You, Lord, for being a forgiving God. Thank You that You are faithful and just to forgive us our sins and to cleanse us from all unrighteousness.[2] Cleanse my daughter. Create in her a pure and clean heart. Cast her not away from Your presence, but renew a right spirit within her. Restore the joy of Your salvation in her life.[3]

Father, please fill _____ with Your peace which passes all understanding.[4] Thank You, Lord, that You are doing a new work in her life.[5] I pray that she will not wallow in self-pity but forget about the past by pressing forward.[6]

Thank You, Lord, for giving my daughter another chance, for You are the God of unconditional love.[7] Thank You, Lord, for being her healer. I speak total restoration over _____ right now. In Jesus' name!

God's Word Says

1. "You [Satan] intended to harm me, but God intended it for good to accomplish what is now being done, the saving of many lives" (Gen. 50:20).

2. "You may ask me for anything in my name, and I will do it" (John 14:14).

3. "Immediately, something like scales fell from Saul's eyes, and he could see again. He got up and was baptized" (Acts 9:18).

4. "For he will command his angels concerning you to guard you in all your ways" (Ps. 91:11).

5. "And we know that in all things God works for the good of those who love him, who have been called according to his purpose" (Rom. 8:28).

6. "For just as the Father raises the dead and gives them life, even so the Son gives life to whom he is pleased to give it" (John 5:21).

31
ABORTION (CONTEMPLATING ONE)

Dear heavenly Father, I praise You because You can take what the enemy meant for bad and turn it around for good.[1] Father, You said if I ask anything according to Your Word You will do it.[2] So grab hold of _____. She's thinking about having an abortion, and I pray, Lord, that You by Your Spirit will stop her. Wake her up, Lord, and take the blinders off her eyes.[3] You're the only One who can. Satan, right now in the name of Jesus Christ I command you to take your hands off of my daughter. Loose her and let her go! She belongs to Jesus.

Thank You, Lord, for causing her to realize the effect this would have on her and the little child she is now carrying. I ask You to protect and nurture the precious little child in her womb.[4] Thank you for working all things out for the good of those who love You.[5] I praise You for moving on her, helping her to choose against an abortion and choosing to let the baby live, for You are the giver of life.[6]

God's Word Says

1. "For he has rescued us from the dominion of darkness and brought us into the kingdom of the Son he loves" (Col. 1:13).

2. "O Lord, you have searched me and you know me. You know when I sit and when I rise; you perceive my thoughts from afar. You discern my going out and my lying down; you are familiar with all my ways" (Ps. 139:1-3).

3. "But because of his great love for us, God, who is rich in mercy, made us alive with Christ even when we were dead in transgressions — it is by grace you have been saved" (Eph. 2:4-5).

4. "Come to me, all you who are weary and burdened, and I will give you rest" (Matt. 11:28).

5. "He heals the brokenhearted and binds up their wounds" (Ps. 147:3).

6. "And the peace of God, which transcends all understanding, will guard your hearts and your minds in Christ Jesus" (Phil. 4:7).

7. "Trust in the Lord forever, for the Lord, the Lord, is the Rock eternal" (Is. 26:4).

8. "Cast all your anxiety on him because he cares for you" (1 Pet. 5:7).

9. "The Lord is far from the wicked but he hears the prayer of the righteous" (Prov. 15:29).

10. "'For I know the plans I have for you,' declares the Lord, 'plans to prosper you and not to harm you, plans to give you hope and a future'" (Jer. 29:11).

32
ABUSE

Father, I break every unclean tie of the past and thank You for setting _____ free from all manipulation.[1]

Father, You know what my child has been through. You have felt his pain, and You have seen his tears.[2] Please wrap Your arms of acceptance around him right now. Surround him with Your love — a kind of love that only comes from You.[3]

Father, You said to come to You when we are heavy laden, and You would give us rest.[4] So I come today, requesting rest for my child. Heal his broken heart.[5] Fill him with Your peace which passes all understanding.[6] Let Your healing virtue and power flow into his mind, healing his emotions. Thank You for being his everlasting strength.[7]

Father, I cast my care upon You because You care for us.[8] Thank You for hearing and answering my prayer.[9] Thank You for restoring my child and giving him a vision for his future.[10] In Jesus' name.

God's Word Says

1. "So is my word that goes out from my mouth: It will not return to me empty, but will accomplish what I desire and achieve the purpose for which I sent it" (Is. 55:11).

2. "I have given you authority to trample on snakes and scorpions and to overcome all the power of the enemy; nothing will harm you" (Luke 10:19).

3. "Then you will know the truth, and the truth will set you free" (John 8:32).

4. "'No weapon forged against you will prevail, and you will refute every tongue that accuses you. This is the heritage of the servants of the Lord, and this is their vindication from me,' declares the Lord" (Is. 54:17).

5. "In addition to all this, take up the shield of faith, with which you can extinguish all the flaming arrows of the evil one" (Eph. 6:16).

6. "So I say, live by the Spirit, and you will not gratify the desires of the sinful nature" (Gal. 5:16).

7. "Submit yourselves, then, to God. Resist the devil, and he will flee from you" (James 4:7).

8. "The Lord is my rock, my fortress and my deliverer; my God is my rock, in whom I take refuge. He is my shield and the horn of my salvation, my stronghold" (Ps. 18.2).

9. "So if the Son sets you free, you will be free indeed" (John 8:36).

33
ADDICTION

Heavenly Father, Your Word does not return void; it will accomplish what You have sent it forth to do.[1] You have given me all authority over the enemy in my child's life, and I command every addictive power to be broken over my child's life.[2] Addictions have no dominion over _____. I praise You that the truth is setting her free.[3] My child is delivered from the bondage of addiction, and no weapon formed against her will prosper.[4] Every fiery dart of addiction is thwarted in her life because of the impenetrable shield of faith.[5] Place a hedge of protection around her, protecting her from any person, place or thing that would tempt her to fall.

I confess that my child will live by the Spirit and will not gratify the desires of the sinful nature.[6] Give her strength to resist the devil so he has to flee.[7] You alone are her rock, rescuer, defense and fortress.[8] I praise You that _____ is completely and totally free from the power of addiction[9] because of her freedom in Christ.

GOD'S WORD SAYS

1. "For nothing is impossible with God" (Luke 1:37).

2. "Jesus went throughout Galilee, teaching in their synagogues, preaching the good news of the kingdom, and healing every disease and sickness among the people" (Matt. 4:23).

3. "Let us then approach the throne of grace with confidence, so that we may receive mercy and find grace to help us in our time of need" (Heb. 4:16).

4. "Jesus Christ is the same yesterday and today and forever" (Heb. 13:8).

5. "He said, "If you listen carefully to the voice of the Lord your God and do what is right in his eyes, if you pay attention to his commands and keep all his decrees, I will not bring on you any of the diseases I brought on the Egyptians, for I am the Lord, who heals you" (Ex. 15:26).

6. "But he was wounded for our transgressions, he was bruised for our iniquities: the chastisement of our peace was upon him; and with his stripes we are healed" (Is. 53:5, KJV).

7. "And if the Spirit of him who raised Jesus from the dead is living in you, he who raised Christ from the dead will also give life to your mortal bodies through his Spirit, who lives in you" (Rom. 8:11).

8. "He gives strength to the weary and increases the power of the weak...but those who hope in the Lord will renew their strength. They will soar on wings like eagles; they will run and not grow weary, they will walk and not be faint" (Is. 40:29,31).

9. "And these signs will accompany those who believe: In my name they will...place their hands on sick people, and they will get well" (Mark 16:17-18).

34
AIDS

Dear heavenly Father, nothing is impossible with You.[1] You can heal every kind of sickness and disease.[2] I praise You because You are a miracle-working God. I come boldly to the throne of grace to find Your grace and mercy in this time of need.[3]

Thank You for being the same yesterday, today and forever.[4] Right now let Your healing virtue and power flow into _____'s body, for You are the Lord our Healer.[5] By Your stripes we were healed.[6]

Satan, I command you to take your hands off my child in Jesus' name! AIDS, I command you to loose my child's body! I command the immune system to line up with the Word of God and be made whole right now in Jesus' name!

The same Spirit that raised Jesus from the dead lives in my son![7] Sickness and disease have no right to live in my son's body. He is strong and healthy in Jesus' name![8] I praise You for giving us Your power over disease.[9]

God's Word Says

1. "Cast all your anxiety on him because he cares for you" (1 Pet. 5:7).

2. "Come to me, all you who are weary and burdened, and I will give you rest. Take my yoke upon you and learn from me, for I am gentle and humble in heart, and you will find rest for your souls" (Matt. 11:28-29).

3. "Peace I leave with you; my peace I give you. I do not give to you as the world gives. Do not let your hearts be troubled and do not be afraid" (John 14:27).

4. "Do not be anxious about anything, but in everything, by prayer and petition, with thanksgiving, present your requests to God. And the peace of God, which transcends all understanding, will guard your hearts and your minds in Christ Jesus" (Phil. 4:6-7).

5. "Trust in the Lord with all your heart and lean not on your own understanding; in all your ways acknowledge him, and he will make your paths straight" (Prov. 3:5-6).

6. "Yet I am always with you; you hold me by my right hand" (Ps. 73:23).

7. "Let the peace of Christ rule* in your hearts, since as members of one body you were called to peace" (Col. 3:15).

* The Hebrew word for *rule, brabeuo,* means "arbitrate," much as an umpire who arbitrates a game of baseball.

35
ANXIETY

I command anxiety to be broken over my child's life right now. I release the peace of God that passes knowledge to guard her heart and mind. Lord, thank You, heavenly Father, because Your thoughts are always focused toward _____, and You are watching everything that concerns her.[1] When my child comes to You, You give her rest. My child wears Your yoke, and it fits perfectly.[2]

Thank You for Your gift of peace. It destroys the bondage of anxiety. That peace isn't fragile like the peace that the world gives, so my child has no reason to be troubled or afraid.[3] Your peace is more wonderful than the human mind can understand, and it keeps my child's thoughts and heart quiet as she trusts in You.[4]

Thank You that my child is trusting You completely and doesn't trust in herself. As a result You will direct her path and crown her every effort with success.[5] Thank You for holding my child by the right hand[6] and allowing Your peace to umpire her heart![7]

GOD'S WORD SAYS

1. "Therefore, if anyone is in Christ, he is a new creation; the old has gone, the new has come!" (2 Cor. 5:17).

2. "And I will do whatever you ask in my name, so that the Son may bring glory to the Father" (John 14:13).

3. "Never be lacking in zeal, but keep your spiritual fervor, serving the Lord" (Rom. 12:11).

4. "We do not want you to become lazy, but to imitate those who through faith and patience inherit what has been promised" (Heb. 6:12).

5. "For it is God who works in you to will and to act according to his good purpose" (Phil. 2:13).

36
APATHY

Father, I bring my child before You as an act of my faith. I thank You for making him a new creation in Christ, causing his old attitudes to pass away.[1] I come against apathy in Jesus' name, knowing that whatever I ask for in His name shall be done.[2]

I pray that You would clothe _____ with spiritual fervor so he can serve You fully.[3] Keep all dullness and indifference from him so that he can receive what You've promised as a result of his faith and patience.[4] Holy Spirit, I invite You to work fully in him, giving him a desire to obey You and to do what You want him to do.[5]

GOD'S WORD SAYS

1. "I will give you a new heart and put a new spirit in you; I will remove from you your heart of stone and give you a heart of flesh" (Ezek. 36:26).

2. "See to it that no one misses the grace of God and that no bitter root grows up to cause trouble and defile many" (Heb. 12:15).

3. "Be kind and compassionate to one another, forgiving each other, just as in Christ God forgave you" (Eph. 4:32).

4. "Therefore, as God's chosen people, holy and dearly loved, clothe yourselves with compassion, kindness, humility, gentleness and patience. Bear with each other and forgive whatever grievances you may have against one another. Forgive as the Lord forgave you. And over all these virtues put on love, which binds them all together in perfect unity. Let the peace of Christ rule in your hearts, since as members of one body you were called to peace. And be thankful. Let the word of Christ dwell in you richly as you teach and admonish one another with all wisdom, and as you sing psalms, hymns and spiritual songs with gratitude in your hearts to God. And whatever you do, whether in word or deed, do it all in the name of the Lord Jesus, giving thanks to God the Father through him" (Col. 3:12-17).

5. "Love is patient, love is kind. It does not envy, it does not boast, it is not proud. It is not rude, it is not self-seeking, it is not easily angered, it keeps no record of wrongs. Love does not delight in evil but rejoices with the truth. It always protects, always trusts, always hopes, always perseveres. Love never fails" (1 Cor. 13:4-8).

37

BITTERNESS

Heavenly Father, I praise You for the anointing of the Holy Spirit that sets my child completely free of all bitterness in her life. Remove _____ 's heart of stone which has kept her in bondage to bitterness, and replace it with a heart of flesh.[1] Then she will not fail to find Your blessings because bitterness will not have taken root in her heart.[2] Make her kind to others, tender and quick to forgive just as You have forgiven her because she belongs to Christ.[3]

Let the peace which comes from Christ be always present in my child's heart and life. Bring to her remembrance the things that Christ taught, and let those words enrich her life and make her wise[4] protecting her heart from every root of bitterness.

Thank You that Your love in her is patient and kind. It is not easily angered, and it keeps no record of wrongs. Your love has been poured out in my child's heart and is powerful. It never fails.[5]

GOD'S WORD SAYS

1. "Reach down your hand from on high; deliver me and rescue me from the mighty waters, from the hands of foreigners whose mouths are full of lies, whose right hands are deceitful" (Ps. 144:7-8).

2. "They must be silenced, because they are ruining whole households by teaching things they ought not to teach — and that for the sake of dishonest gain" (Titus 1:11).

3. "But they will not get very far because, as in the case of those men, their folly will be clear to everyone" (2 Tim. 3:9).

4. "I have given you authority to trample on snakes and scorpions and to overcome all the power of the enemy; nothing will harm you" (Luke 10:19).

5. "The Lord gives sight to the blind, the Lord lifts up those who are bowed down, the Lord loves the righteous" (Ps. 146:8).

6. "And he will go on before the Lord, in the spirit and power of Elijah, to turn the hearts of the fathers to their children and the disobedient to the wisdom of the righteous — to make ready a people prepared for the Lord" (Luke 1:17).

38
CULT INFLUENCE

Lord, I pray that You would reach down Your hand to rescue and deliver _____ from mighty waters that may seem to overtake him. Rescue him from the hands of foreign religions that teach lies and swear by deceitful things.[1]

Silence the ones who are trying to influence him. Keep them from bringing ruin to whole households by false teaching for the sake of dishonest gain.[2] I pray that every cult will fail as their folly becomes clear to everyone around them.[3] I take authority over every evil spirit at work in these false religions, confident in Your power to overcome the enemy![4] Give sight to my child's blind eyes,[5] Lord, and turn him to the wisdom of the righteous.[6]

GOD'S WORD SAYS

1. "So those who have faith are blessed along with Abraham, the man of faith" (Gal. 3:9).

2. "Praise be to the God and Father of our Lord Jesus Christ, who has blessed us in the heavenly realms with every spiritual blessing in Christ" (Eph. 1:3).

3. "But God said to Balaam, 'Do not go with them. You must not put a curse on those people, because they are blessed'" (Num. 22:12).

4. "How can I curse those whom God has not cursed? How can I denounce those whom the Lord has not denounced?" (Num. 23:8).

5. "He wore cursing as his garment; it entered into his body like water, into his bones like oil. May it be like a cloak wrapped about him, like a belt tied forever around him. May this be the Lord's payment to my accusers, to those who speak evil of me. But you, O Sovereign Lord, deal well with me for your name's sake; out of the goodness of your love, deliver me" (Ps. 109:18-21).

6. "Christ redeemed us from the curse of the law by becoming a curse for us, for it is written: 'Cursed is everyone who is hung on a tree'" (Gal. 3:13).

7. "The Lord's curse is on the house of the wicked, but he blesses the home of the righteous" (Prov. 3:33).

39
CURSES

Lord, I thank You for blessing _____ because of her faith just as You mightily blessed Abraham.[1] Thank You for blessing her in the heavenly realms with every spiritual blessing in Christ.[2] Therefore, I know that anyone who tries to curse my child is merely wasting his time — those blessed by God cannot be harmed by a curse![3] How can anyone put a curse on my child when God cannot?[4]

In the name of Jesus I rebuke the one who wears cursing as his garment because God delivered my child by the goodness of His love.[5] Christ redeemed her from the curse of the law by actually becoming a curse for her.[6]

I proclaim a blessing upon our home because You have made us righteous. There is no room for any curse at all![7]

GOD'S WORD SAYS

1. "Surely he took up our infirmities and carried our sorrows, yet we considered him stricken by God, smitten by him, and afflicted" (Is. 53:4).

2. "But may all who seek you rejoice and be glad in you; may those who love your salvation always say, 'The Lord be exalted!'" (Ps. 40:16).

3. "Take the helmet of salvation and the sword of the Spirit, which is the word of God" (Eph. 6:17).

4. "Nehemiah said, 'Go and enjoy choice food and sweet drinks, and send some to those who have nothing prepared. This day is sacred to our Lord. Do not grieve, for the joy of the Lord is your strength'" (Neh. 8:10).

5. "You have made known to me the paths of life; you will fill me with joy in your presence" (Acts 2:28).

6. "From the west, men will fear the name of the Lord, and from the rising of the sun, they will revere his glory. For he will come like a pent-up flood that the breath of the Lord drives along" (Is. 59:19).

7. "And the peace of God, which transcends all understanding, will guard your hearts and your minds in Christ Jesus" (Phil. 4:7).

40
DEPRESSION

Father, thank You for sending Jesus to heal the broken-hearted. Thank You that Jesus took my son's infirmities and carried all of his sorrows.[1] Depression will have no place in his life. I command the spirit of heaviness to be broken and replaced with praise! Because _____ is born of You, I pray that Your joy may be given to him so he can constantly exclaim, "How great God is!"[2] My child knows Your salvation, and the helmet of salvation protects his mind from all emotional manipulation of the devil.[3] Restore the joy of Your salvation to his life. Let him take his eyes off himself and see the needs of the people around him.

The joy of the Lord will give my child strength to resist depression.[4] I know that You will give him back his life, and he will find joy in Your presence.[5] Your power will raise up the standard of joy and strength in my child's life so that the enemy's depressing flood will not triumph.[6] I pray that Your peace will guard and protect his heart and mind.[7]

GOD'S WORD SAYS

1. "I tell you the truth, if anyone says to this mountain, 'Go, throw yourself into the sea,' and does not doubt in his heart but believes that what he says will happen, it will be done for him" (Mark 11:23).

2. "Consequently, faith comes from hearing the message, and the message is heard through the word of Christ" (Rom. 10:17).

3. "In addition to all this, take up the shield of faith, with which you can extinguish all the flaming arrows of the evil one" (Eph. 6:16).

4. "I will give you the keys of the kingdom of heaven; whatever you bind on earth will be bound in heaven, and whatever you loose on earth will be loosed in heaven" (Matt. 16:19).

5. "God is not a man, that he should lie, nor a son of man, that he should change his mind. Does he speak and then not act? Does he promise and not fulfill?" (Num. 23:19).

6. "The one who calls you is faithful and he will do it" (1 Thess. 5:24).

7. "Trust in the Lord with all your heart and lean not on your own understanding" (Prov. 3:5).

8. "We do not want you to become lazy, but to imitate those who through faith and patience inherit what has been promised" (Heb. 6:12).

41

DOUBT

Father, thank You that in Jesus' name doubt has no authority over _____ 's life. You said that if my child has faith and does not doubt, she will be able to command even a mountain into the sea, and it will be done.[1] Her faith comes from listening to the good news about Christ[2] and is a shield to protect her from the fiery darts of the enemy.[3]

You said that whatever is bound on earth will be bound in heaven, and so I bind doubt and the things that have caused doubt in my child's life.[4] My child has every right to take You at Your word, Lord, because You are not prone to lying. Show her that You don't change Your mind as humans do.[5] You will do all You promised to do concerning her.[6] I pray she will trust You with all her heart, not depending on her own limited understanding of who You are and what You have in store for her.[7] Help her to imitate others who have used faith and patience to inherit Your promises.[8]

God's Word Says

1. "Therefore, I urge you, brothers, in view of God's mercy, to offer your bodies as living sacrifices, holy and pleasing to God — this is your spiritual act of worship. Do not conform any longer to the pattern of this world, but be transformed by the renewing of your mind. Then you will be able to test and approve what God's will is — his good, pleasing and perfect will" (Rom. 12:1-2).

2. "The weapons we fight with are not the weapons of the world. On the contrary, they have divine power to demolish strongholds" (2 Cor. 10:4).

3. "The thief cometh not, but for to steal, and to kill, and to destroy: I am come that they might have life, and that they might have it more abundantly" (John 10:10, KJV).

4. "Those who oppose him he must gently instruct, in the hope that God will grant them repentance leading them to a knowledge of the truth, and that they will come to their senses and escape from the trap of the devil, who has taken them captive to do his will" (2 Tim. 2:25-26).

5. "No weapon that is formed against thee shall prosper; and every tongue that shall rise against thee in judgment thou shalt condemn. This is the heritage of the servants of the Lord, and their righteousness is of me, saith the Lord" (Is. 54:17).

6. "Blessed is the man who perseveres under trial, because when he has stood the test, he will receive the crown of life that God has promised to those who love him" (James 1:12).

42

DRUGS AND ALCOHOL

Father, thank You for the yoke-destroying power of God at work in my child's life. With the authority of the Word of God I break the bondage of drugs and alcohol over _____ 's life today. His spirit, soul and body belong to You. May my child's body be used as a living sacrifice, holy and pleasing to You. No longer will he conform to the world and its destructive patterns, but he is being transformed right before my eyes.[1] I have used my spiritual weapon of prayer to demolish strongholds.[2] I will not allow the thief to steal, kill or destroy my child through drugs and alcohol because Jesus purchased abundant life for him.[3]

Thank You for repentance which leads to a clear knowledge of truth and for bringing him to his senses as he escapes the devil's trap.[4] No weapon formed against my son will prosper![5]

Thank You for giving him the power to resist temptation and for the crown of life that is his reward.[6] He whom the Son sets free is free indeed!

GOD'S WORD SAYS

1. "Therefore, I urge you, brothers, in view of God's mercy, to offer your bodies as living sacrifices, holy and pleasing to God — this is your spiritual act of worship" (Rom. 12:1).

2. "Do not conform any longer to the pattern of this world, but be transformed by the renewing of your mind. Then you will be able to test and approve what God's will is — his good, pleasing and perfect will" (Rom. 12:2).

3. "For God has not given us a spirit of fear, but of power and of love and of a sound mind" (2 Tim. 1:7, NKJV).

4. "For they are life to those who find them and health to a man's whole body" (Prov. 4:22).

5. "You belong to your father, the devil, and you want to carry out your father's desire. He was a murderer from the beginning, not holding to the truth, for there is no truth in him. When he lies, he speaks his native language, for he is a liar and the father of lies" (John 8:44).

6. "He called his twelve disciples to him and gave them authority to drive out evil spirits and to heal every disease and sickness" (Matt. 10:1).

7. "Therefore, if anyone is in Christ, he is a new creation; the old has gone, the new has come!" (2 Cor. 5:17).

8. "Stand firm then, with the belt of truth buckled around your waist, with the breastplate of righteousness in place" (Eph. 6:14).

9. "But the Lord said to Samuel, 'Do not consider his appearance or his height, for I have rejected him. The Lord does not look at the things man looks at. Man looks at the outward appearance, but the Lord looks at the heart'" (1 Sam. 16:7).

43
EATING DISORDERS

Heavenly Father, I pray that _____ would present her body as a living sacrifice to You, holy and acceptable.[1] I pray against the stronghold of an eating disorder and thank You in advance that my child's mind is transformed and renewed by Your Word.[2] Your Word assures her of the right to wholeness of mind[3] and a healthy, whole body.[4]

I rebuke the father of all lies and the deceptive thoughts he would try to use against my child's mind and body.[5] I take authority over her destructive disease and over every behavioral pattern associated with it.[6]

My child is a new creation because of Christ, and I proclaim that she will begin to see herself that way.[7] I pray that the belt of truth would be firmly wrapped around her waist so that she finds her balance in what You think of her so she can stand firm.[8] I pray that my child would not be affected by the opinions of those who look on the outward appearance but will see herself as You do because You look on the heart.[9]

God's Word Says

1. "God is our refuge and strength, an ever-present help in trouble. Therefore we will not fear, though the earth give way and the mountains fall into the heart of the sea" (Ps. 46:1-2).

2. "For God did not give us a spirit of timidity, but a spirit of power, of love and of self-discipline" (2 Tim. 1:7).

3. "So we say with confidence, 'The Lord is my helper; I will not be afraid. What can man do to me?'" (Heb. 13:6).

4. "Through Christ Jesus the law of the Spirit of life set me free from the law of sin and death" (Rom. 8:2).

5. "When I am afraid, I will trust in you" (Ps. 56:3).

6. "The wicked man flees though no one pursues, but the righteous are as bold as a lion" (Prov. 28:1).

7. "You are my hiding place; you will protect me from trouble and surround me with songs of deliverance" (Ps. 32:7).

8. "There is no fear in love. But perfect love drives out fear, because fear has to do with punishment. The one who fears is not made perfect in love" (1 John 4:18).

44
FEAR

I command fear to loose its grip from _____ 's life! I rebuke the paralyzing power of fear upon my child.

Thank You that You are a very present help for my child in any time of trouble. He has no need to fear. Even if the mountains were to crumble to the sea[1] You are still his God. Fear is something that is not from You, for You give only power, love and a sound mind.[2] Thank You that my child can say of You, "The Lord is my Helper, and I am not afraid of anything mere man can do to me."[3]

I proclaim that he is free from the law of sin and death[4] and alive to the Spirit of Christ. Whenever my child is tempted to be afraid I ask that You, Father, will help him put his confidence in You.[5] Let my child be bold as a lion.[6] Remind him that You are his hiding place from every storm in life; You even keep him from getting into trouble! You surround him with songs of victory.[7] I pray that my child will experience the realness of Your love and know there is no fear in Your love.[8]

God's Word Says

1. "And the peace of God, which transcends all understanding, will guard your hearts and your minds in Christ Jesus" (Phil. 4:7).

2. "Who shall separate us from the love of Christ? Shall trouble or hardship or persecution or famine or nakedness or danger or sword?...No, in all these things we are more than conquerors through him who loved us" (Rom. 8:35,37).

3. "You belong to your father, the devil, and you want to carry out your father's desire. He was a murderer from the beginning, not holding to the truth, for there is no truth in him. When he lies, he speaks his native language, for he is a liar and the father of lies" (John 8:44).

4. "It is God who works in you to will and to act according to his good purpose" (Phil. 2:13).

5. "For God did not give us a spirit of timidity, but a spirit of power, of love and of self-discipline" (2 Tim. 1:7).

6. "Brothers, I do not consider myself yet to have taken hold of it. But one thing I do: Forgetting what is behind and straining toward what is ahead, I press on toward the goal to win the prize for which God has called me heavenward in Christ Jesus" (Phil. 3:13-14).

45

FEAR OF FAILURE

Lord, I pray that the peace of Christ which is far above all understanding and logic will guard my child's heart and mind against the fear of failure.[1] Thank You for Your promise that nothing shall be able to separate us from Your love which has made us more than conquerors.[2]

I come against Satan, the father of lies.[3] In Jesus' name the lie of failure ceases to be effective in _____ 's life. You are the only One working in her life. You are willing, and You are already acting according to the good purposes You have for her.[4] The attitude of fear in my child is not from You. You have given her an attitude of power, love and a sound mind.[5]

I pray that my child will forget any past failures and shortcomings and strain toward the future things You have in store for her. Give her strength to press on toward the goal to win the prize.[6] Wrap Your arms of encouragement around her. Let her know that with You nothing is impossible. She can do all things through Jesus!

God's Word Says

1. "But the fruit of the Spirit is love, joy, peace, patience, kindness, goodness, faithfulness, gentleness and self-control. Against such things there is no law" (Gal. 5:22-23).

2. "For God did not give us a spirit of timidity, but a spirit of power, of love and of self-discipline" (2 Tim. 1:7).

3. "They will come to their senses and escape from the trap of the devil, who has taken them captive to do his will" (2 Tim. 2:26).

4. "The weapons we fight with are not the weapons of the world. On the contrary, they have divine power to demolish strongholds" (2 Cor. 10:4).

5. "In addition to all this, take up the shield of faith, with which you can extinguish all the flaming arrows of the evil one" (Eph. 6:16).

6. "Have you not put a hedge around him and his household and everything he has? You have blessed the work of his hands, so that his flocks and herds are spread throughout the land" (Job 1:10).

7. "For the love of money is a root of all kinds of evil. Some people, eager for money, have wandered from the faith and pierced themselves with many griefs" (1 Tim. 6:10).

8. "So if the Son sets you free, you will be free indeed" (John 8:36).

46

GAMBLING

Father, thank You that the fruit of the Spirit has been deposited in my child's life. I am asking that the fruit of self-control will manifest in his life.[1] I take authority over the temptation and addiction of gambling. I command it to cease its control over him, so he will know the power, love and self-discipline that comes from You.[2]

I will not allow _____ to be taken captive to do the devil's will.[3] I exercise authority through the weapon of prayer, and I praise You because it is mighty to the pulling down of strongholds.[4] Every fiery dart of gambling is thwarted in my child's life because of the shield of faith which You have given to him.[5]

I pray a hedge of protection around my child from everything that would try to hinder the plan and purpose You have for his life.[6] Father, Your power is free to work in my child's life, delivering him from the love of money which is a root to all kinds of evil.[7] For he who the Son has set free is free indeed![8]

GOD'S WORD SAYS

1. "I pray also that the eyes of your heart may be enlightened in order that you may know the hope to which he has called you, the riches of his glorious inheritance in the saints" (Eph. 1:18).

2. "For our struggle is not against flesh and blood, but against the rulers, against the authorities, against the powers of this dark world and against the spiritual forces of evil in the heavenly realms" (Eph. 6:12).

3. "All who sin apart from the law will also perish apart from the law, and all who sin under the law will be judged by the law" (Rom. 12:2).

4. "I have given you authority to trample on snakes and scorpions and to overcome all the power of the enemy; nothing will harm you" (Luke 10:19).

5. "To the praise of his glorious grace, which he has freely given us in the One he loves" (Eph. 1:6).

6. "Where there is no vision, the people perish: but he that keepeth the law, happy is he" (Prov. 29:18, KJV).

7. "For it is God who works in you to will and to act according to his good purpose" (Phil. 2:13).

47
GANGS

Heavenly Father, thank You that the eyes of my child's understanding are being enlightened to know the hope that only comes from You.[1] I do not fight against the flesh and blood influences in my child's life but against the principalities and powers that have tried to claim authority over my child's destiny.[2] I rebuke the controlling tricks of gangs and gang activities which are used on my child.

I assert that _____ is no longer conforming to the patterns of this world and its false sense of identity but is being transformed right before my very eyes.[3] I take authority over all the power of the enemy, and nothing shall by any means hurt my child![4] Even the powers of hell cannot keep Your love from him.

Thank You for revealing to my child that he is accepted into the family of God through Jesus Christ.[5] He will not cast off restraint and run wild, for You are placing a vision in his heart[6] and are working in him to will and do of Your good pleasure.[7]

God's Word Says

1. "If we confess our sins, he is faithful and just and will forgive us our sins and purify us from all unrighteousness" (1 John 1:9).

2. "As far as the east is from the west, so far has he removed our transgressions from us" (Ps. 103:12).

3. "Let us then approach the throne of grace with confidence, so that we may receive mercy and find grace to help us in our time of need" (Heb. 4:16).

4. "Forget the former things; do not dwell on the past. See, I am doing a new thing!" (Is. 43:18-19).

5. "Therefore, if anyone is in Christ, he is a new creation; the old has gone, the new has come" (2 Cor. 5:17).

6. "Do not conform any longer to the pattern of this world, but be transformed by the renewing of your mind. Then you will be able to test and approve what God's will is — his good, pleasing and perfect will" (Rom. 12:2).

7. "And we, who with unveiled faces all reflect the Lord's glory, are being transformed into his likeness with ever-increasing glory, which comes from the Lord, who is the Spirit" (2 Cor. 3:18).

8. "For you did not receive a spirit that makes you a slave again to fear, but you received the Spirit of sonship. And by him we cry, 'Abba, Father'" (Rom. 8:15).

48
GUILT

Heavenly Father, I praise You for Your never-ending mercy and grace. Thank You that when my child confesses her sins to You, You will forgive and cleanse her from every wrong.[1] You have separated her sin from her as far as the east is from the west.[2] Thank You that _____ has a right to come boldly unto Your throne and stay there to receive mercy and grace for whatever she may need.[3]

I rebuke Satan and the deception he would use to keep my child looking at the past instead of the future.[4] She has become a brand-new person inside. She is not the same anymore; a new life has begun.[5]

I release the mind-renewing power of God over my child today[6] and thank You for the blood of Christ which transforms my child's life, heart and mind into Your image.[7] I proclaim that my child will not cringe or be fearful of You, Lord, but will behave as Your very own child adopted into the bosom of Your family, calling to You, "Father, Father."[8]

GOD'S WORD SAYS

1. "And hope does not disappoint us, because God has poured out his love into our hearts by the Holy Spirit, whom he has given us" (Rom. 5:5).

2. "This is love: not that we loved God, but that he loved us and sent his Son as an atoning sacrifice for our sins" (1 John 4:10).

3. "No one has ever seen God; but if we love one another, God lives in us and his love is made complete in us" (1 John 4:12).

4. "Dear children, let us not love with words or tongue but with actions and in truth" (1 John 3:18-20).

5. "And it shall come to pass in that day, that his burden shall be taken away from off thy shoulder, and his yoke from off thy neck, and the yoke shall be destroyed because of the anointing" (Is. 10:27).

6. "Love never fails. But where there are prophecies, they will cease; where there are tongues, they will be stilled; where there is knowledge, it will pass away" (1 Cor. 13:8).

7. "Whoever loves his brother lives in the light, and there is nothing in him to make him stumble" (1 John 2:10).

8. "For he has rescued us from the dominion of darkness and brought us into the kingdom of the Son he loves" (Col. 1:13).

49
HATE

Thank You for the love of God which has been poured out in my child's heart by the Holy Spirit.[1] Allow her to experience what real love is: not just our earthly love for You but Your supernatural love for us that caused You to send Your Son to satisfy Your anger against our sins.[2] When my child loves other people, You are living in her, and Your love inside of her grows even stronger.[3]

I take authority over hatred in _____ 's heart. Help her to love with actions and in truth, for Your love is made complete in her![4]

Thank You for the burden-removing, yoke-destroying power of God at work in my child's life right now.[5] Thank You for breaking the bondage of hatred with Your perfect love. It never fails.[6] Your love equips my child to walk in the light so she can see her way without stumbling around in darkness and in sin.[7] You have delivered her from the bondage of darkness and translated her into the kingdom of God.[8]

God's Word Says

1. "Because of this, God gave them over to shameful lusts. Even their women exchanged natural relations for unnatural ones" (Rom. 1:26).

2. "For sin shall not be your master, because you are not under law, but under grace" (Rom. 6:14).

3. "For the weapons of our warfare are not carnal, but mighty through God to the pulling down of strong holds" (2 Cor. 10:4).

4. "Take the helmet of salvation and the sword of the Spirit, which is the word of God" (Eph. 6:17).

5. "They exchanged the truth of God for a lie, and worshiped and served created things rather than the Creator — who is forever praised. Amen" (Rom. 1:25).

6. "So is my word that goes out from my mouth: It will not return to me empty, but will accomplish what I desire and achieve the purpose for which I sent it" (Is. 55:11).

7. "For I know that through your prayers and the help given by the Spirit of Jesus Christ, what has happened to me will turn out for my deliverance" (Phil. 1:19).

8. "You belong to your father, the devil, and you want to carry out your father's desire. He was a murderer from the beginning, not holding to the truth, for there is no truth in him. When he lies, he speaks his native language, for he is a liar and the father of lies" (John 8:44).

9. "Then you will know the truth, and the truth will set you free" (John 8:32).

10. "Put on the new self, created to be like God in true righteousness and holiness" (Eph. 4:24).

11. "To the praise of his glorious grace, which he has freely given us in the One he loves" (Eph. 1:6).

50
HOMOSEXUALITY

I come against every perverse spirit that tries to bring my child into sexual bondage.[1] Satan has no authority over _____, for sin will have no dominion over him.[2] My weapon of prayer is a spiritual weapon more powerful than any stronghold in my child's life.[3] I ask that my child's salvation guard his mind from deception just like a helmet.[4]

I release the power of God to move through my child, protecting him from every person, place or thing that would try to pervert the truth of God.[5] Thank You, Father, that Your Word will not return void, but it will fully accomplish what You have sent it forth to do.[6] I have full confidence that my child will be delivered through the Spirit's provision and my prayers.[7] Thank You for giving my child the ability to discern sin and the lies of the devil.[8] Your truth sets him free from the deception of homosexuality.[9] Thank You for restoration, forgiveness and a fresh start.[10] Bring him into the love and acceptance he has been searching for that is found only in Christ.[11]

GOD'S WORD SAYS

1. "For God did not give us a spirit of timidity, but a spirit of power, of love and of self-discipline" (2 Tim. 1:7).

2. "And the peace of God, which transcends all understanding, will guard your hearts and your minds in Christ Jesus" (Phil. 4:7).

3. "And having disarmed the powers and authorities, he made a public spectacle of them, triumphing over them by the cross" (Col. 2:15).

4. "But thanks be to God, who always leads us in triumphal procession in Christ and through us spreads everywhere the fragrance of the knowledge of him" (2 Cor. 2:14).

5. "I will grant peace in the land, and you will lie down and no one will make you afraid. I will remove savage beasts from the land, and the sword will not pass through your country" (Lev. 26:6).

6. "You will be secure, because there is hope; you will look about you and take your rest in safety" (Job 11:18).

7. "But whoever listens to me will live in safety and be at ease, without fear of harm" (Prov. 1:33).

51
INCEST

Thank You for removing fear and the memories that provoke fear from my child. You have replaced her fear with Your healing power, overwhelming love and a rock-solid sound mind.[1] You have given _____ an active peace beyond our understanding to guard her heart and her mind.[2]

Satan, I rebuke you and every demonic attempt to cause my child to be defeated by the tragedy of incest. You are broken, spoiled and powerless, and I stand with Christ to humiliate you openly.[3] My child will be a walking testimony of God's triumph and power.[4]

Thank You, Father, for granting peace that permeates all my child's environment so that even when she sleeps no one can make her afraid.[5] I proclaim that my child is secure, totally stable and filled with tremendous hope. She can rest in the safety she sees surrounding her.[6] My child listens to Your Word and therefore lives in safety and complete ease, without fear of harm.[7]

God's Word Says

1. "They are new every morning; great is your faithfulness" (Lam. 3:23).

2. "I pray that you, being rooted and established in love, may have power, together with all the saints, to grasp how wide and long and high and deep is the love of Christ" (Eph. 3:18).

3. "For if you forgive men when they sin against you, your heavenly Father will also forgive you" (Matt. 6:14).

4. "Blessed are the merciful, for they will be shown mercy" (Matt. 5:7).

5. "Praise be to the God and Father of our Lord Jesus Christ, the Father of compassion and the God of all comfort, who comforts us in all our troubles, so that we can comfort those in any trouble with the comfort we ourselves have received from God" (2 Cor. 1:3-4).

6. "Then I heard a loud voice in heaven say: 'Now have come the salvation and the power and the kingdom of our God, and the authority of his Christ. For the accuser of our brothers, who accuses them before our God day and night, has been hurled down'" (Rev. 12:10).

7. "I will give you a new heart and put a new spirit in you; I will remove from you your heart of stone and give you a heart of flesh" (Ezek. 36:26).

8. "And the Lord answered me, and said, Write the vision, and make it plain upon tables, that he may run that readeth it" (Hab. 2:2, KJV).

9. "Blessed is the man who does not walk in the counsel of the wicked or stand in the way of sinners or sit in the seat of mockers" (Ps. 1:1).

10. "Therefore, as God's chosen people, holy and dearly loved, clothe yourselves with compassion, kindness, humility, gentleness and patience" (Col. 3:12).

52

JUDGMENTAL ATTITUDES

Heavenly Father, thank You for the complete forgiveness and mercy which You show us anew every morning.[1] I pray that _____ will have a full understanding of how high and deep and wide Your love is,[2] so that in turn he may show mercy to others.[3] As he sows mercy he will reap mercy.[4]

I take authority over a judgmental and critical spirit in my child right now and release Your nature and character as the Father of compassion to have free course in him.[5] My child does not take after the devil who is nothing but an accuser.[6]

Remove his critical heart of stone, and replace it with a heart of flesh.[7] I ask that he will become so busy running after his vision[8] that he won't have time to sit in the seat of judgment.[9] Thank You for clothing my child with compassion, mercy, kindness, humility, gentleness and patience.[10]

God's Word Says

1. "We do not want you to become lazy, but to imitate those who through faith and patience inherit what has been promised" (Heb. 6:12).

2. "If a man is lazy, the rafters sag; if his hands are idle, the house leaks" (Eccl. 10:18).

3. "I will give you the keys of the kingdom of heaven; whatever you bind on earth will be bound in heaven, and whatever you loose on earth will be loosed in heaven" (Matt. 16:19).

4. "Diligent hands will rule, but laziness ends in slave labor" (Prov. 12:24).

5. "Never be lacking in zeal, but keep your spiritual fervor, serving the Lord" (Rom. 12:11).

6. "Therefore, my dear friends, as you have always obeyed — not only in my presence, but now much more in my absence — continue to work out your salvation with fear and trembling, for it is God who works in you to will and to act according to his good purpose" (Phil. 2:12-13).

53

LAZINESS

Heavenly Father, I proclaim that _____ ceases to be spiritually bored or indifferent and will excitedly follow the example of those believers who received all You promised because of their strong faith and patience.[1]

I take authority over the laziness that has tried to rot my child's foundation like a leaky roof.[2] You said whatever we bind on earth would be bound in the heavenly realms, and so in the name of Jesus I bind a complacent and apathetic attitude in my child.[3] I pray You will thwart the lazy habits that have begun in her so that she will work hard to become a leader.[4]

I pray that my child would not be lazy in her work but would serve You enthusiastically with a fervent heart.[5] You are at work in her, helping her to want to obey You and putting her to action for Your good purposes.[6]

GOD'S WORD SAYS

1. "God made him who had no sin to be sin for us, so that in him we might become the righteousness of God" (2 Cor. 15:21).

2. "I can do everything through him who gives me strength" (Phil. 4:13).

3. "You belong to your father, the devil, and you want to carry out your father's desire. He was a murderer from the beginning, not holding to the truth, for there is no truth in him. When he lies, he speaks his native language, for he is a liar and the father of lies" (John 8:44).

4. "But you are a chosen people, a royal priesthood, a holy nation, a people belonging to God, that you may declare the praises of him who called you out of darkness into his wonderful light" (1 Pet. 2:9).

5. "For everything that was written in the past was written to teach us, so that through endurance and the encouragement of the Scriptures we might have hope. May the God who gives endurance and encouragement give you a spirit of unity among yourselves as you follow Christ Jesus" (Rom. 15:4-5).

6. "'For I know the plans I have for you,' declares the Lord, 'plans to prosper you and not to harm you, plans to give you hope and a future'" (Jer. 29:11).

54
LOW SELF-ESTEEM

Heavenly Father, thank You for pouring Your goodness into my child so that he takes on Your very character.[1] I pray that _____ will find his self-worth in You, knowing that he can do anything and everything through the strength that Christ gives.[2]

I rebuke the father of lies who has deceived my child to believe he's not worthy to be highly esteemed.[3] I pray that Your love will break through, proving to him that he has been chosen by You as a priest of the King, holy and pure, one of Your very own. Let him be an example to others of how You called him out of darkness into Your marvelous light.[4] Wrap Your arms of encouragement around him, and Your Word is the Word of encouragement.[5]

Thank You for the thoughts You continually have for him. Encourage him by proving the plans You have to prosper him and not to harm him. Show him that You are planning a glorious and hopeful future for him![6]

GOD'S WORD SAYS

1. "Flesh gives birth to flesh, but the Spirit gives birth to spirit" (John 3:6).

2. "Those who live according to the sinful nature have their minds set on what that nature desires; but those who live in accordance with the Spirit have their minds set on what the Spirit desires" (Rom. 8:5).

3. "Therefore each of you must put off falsehood and speak truthfully to his neighbor, for we are all members of one body" (Eph. 4:25).

4. "Surely you desire truth in the inner parts; you teach me wisdom in the inmost place" (Ps. 51:6).

5. "My mouth speaks what is true, for my lips detest wickedness" (Prov. 8:7).

6. "Then you will know the truth, and the truth will set you free" (John 8:32).

55
LYING

Heavenly Father, thank You that my child has been born of Your Spirit and has You living within.[1] I pray that You will bring to her remembrance how to live in accordance with Your Spirit and how to speak as the Spirit desires her to speak.[2]

Make Your Word known even more clearly to _____, Lord. You said we are a part of each other, and when we lie to each other we only hurt ourselves.[3]

Lord, You deserve honesty, straight from the heart. You deserve utter sincerity and truthfulness, and so I take authority over the habit of lying, in Jesus' name.[4] I pray that everything my child says will be measured against truth and that she will hate lies and every deception.[5] May she know the truth, practice the truth and desire the truth — truth to set her free.[6]

GOD'S WORD SAYS

1. "For the word of God is living and active. Sharper than any double-edged sword, it penetrates even to dividing soul and spirit, joints and marrow; it judges the thoughts and attitudes of the heart" (Heb. 4:12).

2. "On the contrary, we speak as men approved by God to be entrusted with the gospel. We are not trying to please men but God, who tests our hearts" (1 Thess. 2:4).

3. "The acts of the sinful nature are obvious: sexual immorality, impurity and debauchery; idolatry and witchcraft; hatred, discord, jealousy, fits of rage, selfish ambition, dissensions, factions and envy; drunkenness, orgies, and the like. I warn you, as I did before, that those who live like this will not inherit the kingdom of God" (Gal. 5:19-21).

4. "Turn my heart toward your statutes and not toward selfish gain" (Ps. 119:36).

5. "Teach me your way, O Lord, and I will walk in your truth; give me an undivided heart, that I may fear your name" (Ps. 86:11).

6. "Finally, brothers, whatever is true, whatever is noble, whatever is right, whatever is pure, whatever is lovely, whatever is admirable — if anything is excellent or praiseworthy — think about such things" (Phil. 4:8).

56
MANIPULATION

Heavenly Father, remove selfish motivations or hidden intentions from my child. May the Word be sharper than a two-edged sword in her life, judging the thoughts and attitudes of her heart.[1] Remind _____ that she should try to please You alone, not men, because You test our hearts.[2]

In the name of Jesus I take authority over selfish ambitions in my child, which are an act of her sinful nature.[3] Turn her heart toward Your goals and objectives and away from selfish gain.[4]

Make my child's heart undivided in motives, Lord, so she may worship Your name.[5] I rebuke the devil from her life and proclaim that my child will think about and act upon things that are true, noble, right, pure, lovely and admirable.[6] In Jesus' name.

God's Word Says

1. "Jesus replied: 'Love the Lord your God with all your heart and with all your soul and with all your mind'" (Matt. 22:37).

2. "Do not offer the parts of your body to sin, as instruments of wickedness, but rather offer yourselves to God, as those who have been brought from death to life; and offer the parts of your body to him as instruments of righteousness" (Rom. 6:13).

3. "Do you not know that your bodies are members of Christ himself? Shall I then take the members of Christ and unite them with a prostitute? Never" (1 Cor. 6:15).

4. "But thanks be to God! He gives us the victory through our Lord Jesus Christ" (1 Cor. 15:57).

5. "Submit yourselves, then, to God. Resist the devil, and he will flee from you" (James 4:7).

6. "Do not conform any longer to the pattern of this world, but be transformed by the renewing of your mind. Then you will be able to test and approve what God's will is — his good, pleasing and perfect will" (Rom. 12:2).

7. "Put to death, therefore, whatever belongs to your earthly nature: sexual immorality, impurity, lust, evil desires and greed, which is idolatry" (Col. 3:5).

8. "Those who belong to Christ Jesus have crucified the sinful nature with its passions and desires" (Gal. 5:24).

9. "What a wretched man I am! Who will rescue me from this body of death?" (Rom. 7:24).

57

MASTURBATION

Heavenly Father, let your Spirit burn in my child's heart. May he love You with all of his heart, soul, mind and strength.[1] I pray he will not use his body as a tool for sin but give himself to You as a tool for You to use for Your good purposes.[2] Remind _____ that his body is actually one of the parts and members of Christ.[3]

I rebuke the devil, refusing to let sin hold my child captive any longer through habitual masturbation. Give him victory over every area of sin and death through Christ Jesus.[4]

I pray he will give himself humbly to You, Lord, acknowledging his reliance on Your goodness and mercy. When he resists the devil, the devil has to flee.[5] My child is no longer conformed to this world and its fleshly desires but is transformed — winning the battle in his mind.[6]

Thank You that he is dead to the evil desires lurking within him.[7] His fleshly desires are nailed to the cross.[8] Rescue him from his body of death.[9]

God's Word Says

1. "The Spirit himself testifies with our spirit that we are God's children" (Rom. 8:16).

2. "It teaches us to say 'No' to ungodliness and worldly passions, and to live self-controlled, upright and godly lives in this present age" (Titus 2:12).

3. "Finally, brothers, whatever is true, whatever is noble, whatever is right, whatever is pure, whatever is lovely, whatever is admirable — if anything is excellent or praiseworthy — think about such things" (Phil. 4:8).

4. "I will set before my eyes no vile thing" (Ps. 101:3)

5. "He who walks righteously and speaks what is right, who...shuts his eyes against contemplating evil — this is the man who will dwell on the heights, whose refuge will be the mountain fortress. His bread will be supplied, and water will not fail him" (Is. 33:15-16).

58
MOVIES

Heavenly Father, I thank You for giving my daughter Your Holy Spirit. She bears witness with her own spirit,[1] causing her to say no to ungodly entertainment so that our rules only reinforce a rock-solid conviction and commitment that she has already made to You.[2]

Give _____ the strength, when we're not around, to choose movies that promote good, clean thoughts.[3] I pray that my child will make You the Lord of her life in this area. Make her determined to allow no vile thing to enter her spirit through her eyes.[4] Help her to walk righteously, speak what is right and shut her eyes from evil temptations.[5] In the name of Jesus.

GOD'S WORD SAYS

1. "Those who live according to the sinful nature have their minds set on what that nature desires; but those who live in accordance with the Spirit have their minds set on what the Spirit desires" (Rom. 8:5).

2. "Do not let any unwholesome talk come out of your mouths, but only what is helpful for building others up according to their needs, that it may benefit those who listen" (Eph. 4:29).

3. "Just as the living Father sent me and I live because of the Father, so the one who feeds on me will live because of me" (John 6:57).

4. "Do not conform any longer to the pattern of this world, but be transformed by the renewing of your mind. Then you will be able to test and approve what God's will is — his good, pleasing and perfect will" (Rom. 12:2).

5. "Finally, brothers, whatever is true, whatever is noble, whatever is right, whatever is pure, whatever is lovely, whatever is admirable — if anything is excellent or praiseworthy — think about such things" (Phil. 4:8).

6. "Do not be misled: 'Bad company corrupts good character'" (1 Cor. 15:33).

7. "The Spirit himself testifies with our spirit that we are God's children" (Rom. 8:16).

59
MUSIC

Heavenly Father, thank You that you are working in
_____'s life. You are placing in him a desire to listen to
and think about music that is in accordance with Your Spirit.
Thank You for causing him to enjoy music that will edify
him and build him up.² I pray that he will feed on music that
portrays Jesus, enjoying and knowing Your kind of life as a
result.³

Thank You, Lord, for the renewing work of Christian
music on my child's mind, transforming him day by day.⁴ I
pray that he would meditate on music
that portrays things which are
true, noble, right, pure,
lovely, admirable, excellent
and praiseworthy.⁵

Thank You for surrounding
_____ with godly influ-
ences⁶ and giving him Your Holy
Spirit to bear witness with his own spirit.⁷ Your
Spirit causes him to say no to ungodly music. Thank You for
building in him a rock-solid conviction to listen to godly
music. In Jesus' name.

God's Word Says

1. "They overcame him by the blood of the Lamb and by the word of their testimony; they did not love their lives so much as to shrink from death" (Rev. 12:11).

2. "He called his twelve disciples to him and gave them authority to drive out evil spirits and to heal every disease and sickness" (Matt. 10:1).

3. "Submit yourselves, then, to God. Resist the devil, and he will flee from you" (James 4:7).

4. "You, dear children, are from God and have overcome them, because the one who is in you is greater than the one who is in the world" (1 John 4:40).

5. "They replied, 'Believe in the Lord Jesus, and you will be saved — you and your household'" (Acts 16:31).

6. "For he has rescued us from the dominion of darkness and brought us into the kingdom of the Son he loves" (Col. 1:13).

7. "'No weapon forged against you will prevail, and you will refute every tongue that accuses you. This is the heritage of the servants of the Lord, and this is their vindication from me,' declares the Lord" (Is. 54:17).

8. "And having disarmed the powers and authorities, he made a public spectacle of them, triumphing over them by the cross" (Col. 2:15).

9. "For our struggle is not against flesh and blood, but against the rulers, against the authorities, against the powers of this dark world and against the spiritual forces of evil in the heavenly realms" (Eph. 6:12).

60
THE OCCULT

Satan, I bind you and every deceptive device of occult activity you have tried to use on my child. I plead the blood of Jesus over _____, knowing that we overcome by the blood of the Lamb and the word of our testimony.[1] The Lord has given me the authority over evil spirits and their hold on her.[2] They have to flee![3]

Father, You are stronger than any evil or wickedness in this world,[4] and You have declared that my household shall be saved.[5] Thank You for rescuing my daughter from the dominion of darkness and bringing her into the kingdom of Your Son.[6] No weapon used against my child will prosper, in Jesus' name.[7]

You have taken away Satan's power and openly displayed Christ's triumph on the cross.[8] Satan and any influences of the occult are defeated from her life! I do not wrestle against flesh and blood influences but against the rulers, authorities and powers of this dark world and against spiritual forces of evil in the heavenly realms.[9]

GOD'S WORD SAYS

1. "In your anger do not sin: Do not let the sun go down while you are still angry" (Eph. 4:26).

2. "But I tell you: Love your enemies and pray for those who persecute you, that you may be sons of your Father in heaven. He causes his sun to rise on the evil and the good, and sends rain on the righteous and the unrighteous" (Matt. 5:44-45).

3. "Be imitators of God, therefore, as dearly loved children and live a life of love, just as Christ loved us and gave himself up for us as a fragrant offering and sacrifice to God" (Eph. 5:1-2).

4. "A man's wisdom gives him patience; it is to his glory to overlook an offense" (Prov. 19:110).

5. "Do not be overcome by evil, but overcome evil with good" (Rom. 12:21).

6. "Be kind and compassionate to one another, forgiving each other, just as in Christ God forgave you" (Eph. 4:32).

61
OFFENSES

Heavenly Father, I pray that _____ would refrain from nursing his grudges.[1] May he love his enemies and pray for the people who persecute him. Help him to act as a true child of heaven.[2] Just as a child imitates his earthly father may he follow Your example in everything he does. Fill him with love for others. May Christ, who gave Himself as a sacrifice, be his ultimate example.[3]

Your Word says that a wise man overlooks insults.[4] I pray You will make my child wise in this manner. I come against foolish pride which causes him to take offense. Thank You that evil will not get the upper hand. Instead I confess You are moving on my child to conquer evil with good.[5]

Thank You that each day my child is overcoming the desire to be offended. Your power is working in him to be kind to others, tenderhearted and forgiving just as God has forgiven those who belong to Christ.[6]

GOD'S WORD SAYS

1. "We demolish arguments and every pretension that sets itself up against the knowledge of God, and we take captive every thought to make it obedient to Christ" (2 Cor. 10:5).

2. "Have nothing to do with the fruitless deeds of darkness, but rather expose them" (Eph. 5:11).

3. "Finally, brothers, whatever is true, whatever is noble, whatever is right, whatever is pure, whatever is lovely, whatever is admirable — if anything is excellent or praiseworthy — think about such things" (Phil. 4:8).

4. "I will set before my eyes no vile thing. The deeds of faithless men I hate; they will not cling to me" (Ps. 101:3).

5. "I made a covenant with my eyes not to look lustfully at a girl" (Job 31:1).

6. "How can a young man keep his way pure? By living according to your word" (Ps. 119:9).

7. "'Food for the stomach and the stomach for food' — but God will destroy them both. The body is not meant for sexual immorality, but for the Lord, and the Lord for the body" (1 Cor. 6:13).

62

PORNOGRAPHY

I come against the stronghold of pornography in my child's life and demolish every imagination that sets itself up against the knowledge of God. I pray that _____ will take every thought captive bringing each thought into the obedience of Christ.[1] She will resist and expose worthless deeds of darkness.[2]

Remove every unclean seed of the past that has been sown in her mind. Let her thoughts be fixed on You as she thinks on things that are true, good, right, lovely and pure.[3] She will put no vile thing before her eyes.[4]

Father, I ask that she will make a covenant with her eyes not to look lustfully at the opposite sex.[5] May she understand the purity of sex within a covenantal marriage relationship. Thank You that my child can stay pure in a perverse world by hiding Your Word in her heart and following its rules.[6] Burn into my child's spirit the knowledge that sexual sin is never right. May she purpose that her body will be filled with You.[7]

God's Word Says

1. "As for you, the anointing you received from him remains in you, and you do not need anyone to teach you. But as his anointing teaches you about all things and as that anointing is real, not counterfeit — just as it has taught you, remain in him" (1 John 2:27).

2. "There is neither Jew nor Greek, slave nor free, male nor female, for you are all one in Christ Jesus" (Gal. 3:28).

3. "There should be no division in the body, but that its parts should have equal concern for each other" (1 Cor. 12:25).

4. "And hope does not disappoint us, because God has poured out his love into our hearts by the Holy Spirit, whom he has given us" (Rom. 5:5).

5. "Love does not delight in evil but rejoices with the truth. It always protects, always trusts, always hopes, always perseveres" (1 Cor. 13:6-7).

6. "So if the Son sets you free, you will be free indeed" (John 8:36).

7. "'Do not go about spreading slander among your people. 'Do not do anything that endangers your neighbor's life. I am the Lord. 'Do not hate your brother in your heart. Rebuke your neighbor frankly so you will not share in his guilt. 'Do not seek revenge or bear a grudge against one of your people, but love your neighbor as yourself. I am the Lord" (Lev. 19:16-18).

63

PREJUDICE

Heavenly Father, thank You for teaching my child all things[1] and revealing to him that there is neither Jew nor Greek, slave nor free, male nor female in the kingdom of God. We are one in Christ.[2] Help _____ to have equal concern for all his brothers and sisters in Christ, empathizing with those who suffer and honoring other people.[3]

Thank You for pouring out Your love into my child's heart by the Holy Spirit,[4] replacing all prejudice. Help my child to show Your love by rejoicing in the truth — not delighting in evil. I pray that Your love in him will always protect, trust and persevere when he considers people of other races.[5]

My child is free from the bondage of prejudice.[6] He does not spread slander among his friends or hate other people in his heart. He does not seek revenge against others or bear any grudges in the name of prejudice or otherwise.[7]

God's Word Says

1. "By the seventh day God had finished the work he had been doing; so on the seventh day he rested from all his work" (Gen. 2:2).

2. "The Lord God took the man and put him in the Garden of Eden to work it and take care of it" (Gen. 2:15).

3. "Lazy hands make a man poor, but diligent hands bring wealth" (Prov. 10:4).

4. "The Lord will send a blessing on your barns and on everything you put your hand to. The Lord your God will bless you in the land he is giving you" (Deut. 28:8).

5. "For who has known the mind of the Lord that he may instruct him? But we have the mind of Christ" (1 Cor. 2:16).

6. "It is because of him that you are in Christ Jesus, who has become for us wisdom from God — that is, our righteousness, holiness and redemption" (1 Cor. 1:30).

7. "All hard work brings a profit, but mere talk leads only to poverty" (Prov. 14:23).

64

PROCRASTINATION

Heavenly Father, thank You for making my child diligent in everything she does. I rebuke procrastination, which is a form of laziness in her life. By Your example, model for her the principle of taking rest *after* the work is finished instead of putting work off to rest.[1] You made us to work naturally[2] and promised to bless the hand of the diligent.[3] Father, proclaim a blessing upon everything to which _____ sets her hand.[4]

You have given my child the mind of Christ,[5] and Christ has been made wisdom for my child.[6] My child will approach every task with wisdom. Thank You for rewarding all of my child's hard work and preventing her from merely talking about working hard.[7]

GOD'S WORD SAYS

1. "I have given you authority to trample on snakes and scorpions and to overcome all the power of the enemy; nothing will harm you" (Luke 10:19).

2. "I have written you in my letter not to associate with sexually immoral people" (1 Cor. 5:9).

3. "Have you not put a hedge around him and his household and everything he has? You have blessed the work of his hands, so that his flocks and herds are spread throughout the land" (Job 1:10).

4. "Above all else, guard your heart, for it is the wellspring of life" (Prov. 4:23).

5. "Don't you know that you yourselves are God's temple and that God's Spirit lives in you?" (1 Cor. 3:16).

6. "Don't let anyone look down on you because you are young, but set an example for the believers in speech, in life, in love, in faith and in purity" (1 Tim. 4:12).

7. "But he who unites himself with the Lord is one with him in spirit. Flee from sexual immorality. All other sins a man commits are outside his body, but he who sins sexually sins against his own body. Do you not know that your body is a temple of the Holy Spirit, who is in you, whom you have received from God? You are not your own; you were bought at a price. Therefore honor God with your body" (1 Cor. 6:17-20).

65

PROMISCUITY

Heavenly Father, thank You for the authority I have over the enemy who would try to put my child in bondage to promiscuity.[1] I break every ungodly tie that _____ may have with another person so that he will not keep company with sexually immoral persons.[2] Put a hedge of protection around him[3] to guard his affections toward the opposite sex. Such affection will influence everything in his life.[4]

Remind him that his interactions with others reflect upon Your dwelling place — the body of Christ.[5] Cause him to be an example to others by his conduct and teaching.[6]

Thank You, Lord, for delivering him from promiscuity to be joined to You. I pray that he will run from sexual sins so that he does not offend his own body which belongs to You.[7] In Jesus' name.

God's Word Says

1. "For sin shall not be your master, because you are not under law, but under grace" (Rom. 6:14).

2. "But Samuel replied: 'Does the Lord delight in burnt offerings and sacrifices as much as in obeying the voice of the Lord? To obey is better than sacrifice, and to heed is better than the fat of rams" (1 Sam. 15:22).

3. "Remind the people to be subject to rulers and authorities, to be obedient, to be ready to do whatever is good" (Titus 3:1).

4. "Listen, my son, to your father's instruction and do not forsake your mother's teaching" (Prov. 1:8).

5. "'If you are willing and obedient, you will eat the best from the land; but if you resist and rebel, you will be devoured by the sword.' For the mouth of the Lord has spoken" (Is. 1:19-20).

6. "I will give you the keys of the kingdom of heaven; whatever you bind on earth will be bound in heaven, and whatever you loose on earth will be loosed in heaven" (Matt. 16:19).

7. "The reason I wrote you was to see if you would stand the test and be obedient in everything" (2 Cor. 2:9).

8. "We demolish arguments and every pretension that sets itself up against the knowledge of God, and we take captive every thought to make it obedient to Christ" (2 Cor. 10:5).

66

REBELLION

Heavenly Father, thank You that rebellion is broken in _____ according to Your Word. Sin will not be my child's master because she is under grace.[1] Obedience is far better than sacrifice,[2] and I pray that _____ will have an obedient attitude toward her teachers, the law, myself and all who are in authority over her.[3] Thank You that my child is not a fool who refuses to be taught.[4] She is obedient, enjoying the very best You have for her. In Jesus' name she will not be devoured by strife like those who resist and rebel.[5]

I bind rebellion in my child's life and thank You that You said whatever is bound in the natural would also be bound in the spiritual.[6] I proclaim that my child will stand the tests to come, being obedient in everything.[7] Let it start in her attitude as she brings every thought into captivity and obedience to Christ.[8]

God's Word Says

1. "My words come from an upright heart; my lips sincerely speak what I know" (Job 33:3).

2. "You were taught, with regard to your former way of life, to put off your old self, which is being corrupted by its deceitful desires; to be made new in the attitude of your minds; and to put on the new self, created to be like God in true righteousness and holiness. Therefore each of you must put off falsehood and speak truthfully to his neighbor, for we are all members of one body" (Eph. 4:22-25).

3. "The tongue also is a fire, a world of evil among the parts of the body. It corrupts the whole person, sets the whole course of his life on fire, and is itself set on fire by hell" (James 3:6).

4. "Nor should there be obscenity, foolish talk or coarse joking, which are out of place, but rather thanksgiving" (Eph. 5:4).

5. "Listen, for I have worthy things to say; I open my lips to speak what is right. My mouth speaks what is true, for my lips detest wickedness" (Prov. 8:6-7).

67

SARCASM

Heavenly Father, may my child's words come from an upright heart.[1] May he be made new in the attitude of his mind.[2]

In Jesus' name I bind the wrong attitudes that promote sarcasm. I proclaim that _____ puts on his new self, created to be like God in true righteousness and holiness. I proclaim that he puts off all falsehood and speaks truthfully in every way to others.[2] My child's tongue will not cause him to become corrupt nor will it set his life on fire.[3]

With the power of the Holy Spirit keep my child from foolish talk or coarse joking with other people. Make his words kind and full of thanksgiving.[4] I pray that other people will listen to him because he has worthy things to say, and he opens his mouth only to speak what is right and true.[5]

GOD'S WORD SAYS

1. "Therefore, if anyone is in Christ, he is a new creation; the old has gone, the new has come!" (2 Cor. 5:17).

2. "How much more, then, will the blood of Christ, who through the eternal Spirit offered himself unblemished to God, cleanse our consciences from acts that lead to death, so that we may serve the living God!" (Heb. 9:14).

3. "I have given you authority to trample on snakes and scorpions and to overcome all the power of the enemy; nothing will harm you" (Luke 10:19).

4. "Forget the former things; do not dwell on the past" (Is. 43:18).

5. "For we do not have a high priest who is unable to sympathize with our weaknesses, but we have one who has been tempted in every way, just as we are — yet was without sin. Let us then approach the throne of grace with confidence, so that we may receive mercy and find grace to help us in our time of need" (Heb. 4:15-16).

6. "You, dear children, are from God and have overcome them, because the one who is in you is greater than the one who is in the world" (1 John 4:4).

68

SEXUAL TIES

Heavenly Father, thank You for making my child a new creation in You! She no longer has to worry about the past mistakes she's made, but she can concentrate on the new things You're doing in her life.[1] I break every worldly tie through the blood of Jesus.[2] I declare freedom from bondage for _____, freedom from all ungodly relationships, including sexual ones. The enemy is defeated in her life because of the authority Christ has given.[3]

Thank You, Father, for renewing her mind, allowing her to forget the former things and not dwell on the past.[4] Remind her that You are our perfect High Priest who understands our weaknesses. Teach my child to be unyielding to temptation. May she come boldly to Your throne and stay there to receive mercy and grace to help her in her time of need.[5]

You live within my child, and You are far greater than any other influence of the world. My child rises as a victor.[6] In Jesus' name!

God's Word Says

1. "So is my word that goes out from my mouth: It will not return to me empty, but will accomplish what I desire and achieve the purpose for which I sent it" (Is. 55:11).

2. "He sent forth his word and healed them; he rescued them from the grave" (Ps. 107:20).

3. "The weapons we fight with are not the weapons of the world. On the contrary, they have divine power to demolish strongholds" (2 Cor. 10:4).

4. "And having disarmed the powers and authorities, he made a public spectacle of them, triumphing over them by the cross" (Col. 2:15).

5. "He himself bore our sins in his body on the tree, so that we might die to sins and live for righteousness; by his wounds you have been healed" (1 Pet. 2:24).

6. "He said, 'If you listen carefully to the voice of the Lord your God and do what is right in his eyes, if you pay attention to his commands and keep all his decrees, I will not bring on you any of the diseases I brought on the Egyptians, for I am the Lord, who heals you'" (Ex. 15:26).

7. "Through Christ Jesus the law of the Spirit of life set me free from the law of sin and death" (Rom. 8:2).

8. "The thief comes only to steal and kill and destroy; I have come that they may have life, and have it to the full" (John 10:10).

69

SICKNESS AND DISEASE

I confess Your Word over my child concerning healing, knowing that Your Word cannot return void. It's accomplishing what it was sent to do,[1] and You've sent it to heal him.[2] The weapons I fight with have divine power in the heavenly realms to demolish the stronghold of sickness and disease in my child's life.[3]

Lord Jesus, thank You for disarming the power and authority of the devil, making a public show of his defeat.[4] You personally carried the load of _____'s sins in Your own body when You died on the cross, so he can be finished with sin and know healing as a lifestyle through Your wounds.[5] I pray that my child will know You as *Jehovah-Rapha*, the Lord, his healer.[6]

Jesus has redeemed my child from sickness and every part of the law of sin and death.[7] My child will not be stolen, killed or destroyed by sickness and disease, because Jesus came to give him life and life abundantly.[8]

GOD'S WORD SAYS

1. "They overcame him by the blood of the Lamb and by the word of their testimony; they did not love their lives so much as to shrink from death" (Rev. 12:11).

2. "Yet this I call to mind and therefore I have hope: Because of the Lord's great love we are not consumed, for his compassions never fail. They are new every morning; great is your faithfulness. I say to myself, 'The Lord is my portion; therefore I will wait for him'" (Lam. 3:21-24).

3. "The thief comes only to steal and kill and destroy; I have come that they may have life, and have it to the full" (John 10:10).

4. "Finally, be strong in the Lord and in his mighty power. Put on the full armor of God so that you can take your stand against the devil's schemes" (Eph. 6:10-11).

5. "As a father has compassion on his children, so the Lord has compassion on those who fear him" (Ps. 103:13).

6. "Neither height nor depth, nor anything else in all creation, will be able to separate us from the love of God that is in Christ Jesus our Lord" (Rom. 8:39).

7. "And provide for those who grieve in Zion — to bestow on them a crown of beauty instead of ashes, the oil of gladness instead of mourning, and a garment of praise instead of a spirit of despair. They will be called oaks of righteousness, a planting of the Lord for the display of his splendor" (Is. 61:3).

70
SUICIDE

Heavenly Father, I thank You that my child defeats the power of the enemy by the blood of the Lamb and by the word of her testimony.[1] I rebuke the spirit of suicide and depression over my child. _____'s mind will be filled with hope as she recalls Your great love and compassion. Cause her to awake each morning with a fresh revelation of Your love and not to be consumed with hopelessness.[2] Let my child experience life in all its fullness, thwarting the enemy's attempt to steal, kill or destroy her.[3]

I pray that my child's strength would come from Your mighty power within her. Thank You for the full armor of God enabling her to stand safe against all strategies and tricks of Satan.[4]

Thank You for Your peace that goes beyond every experience my child has.[5] Cause my child to know that nothing can separate her from Your love![6] I praise You that the spirit of heaviness is broken, and she is now clothed with the garment of praise![7]

God's Word Says

1. "Your word is a lamp to my feet and a light for my path" (Ps. 119:105).

2. "I will set before my eyes no vile thing. The deeds of faithless men I hate; they will not cling to me" (Ps. 101:3).

3. "Through him and for his name's sake, we received grace and apostleship to call people from among all the Gentiles to the obedience that comes from faith" (Rom. 1:5).

4. "Turn my eyes away from worthless things; preserve my life according to your word" (Ps. 119:37).

5. "The sluggard buries his hand in the dish; he is too lazy to bring it back to his mouth" (Prov. 26:15).

6. "We do not want you to become lazy, but to imitate those who through faith and patience inherit what has been promised" (Heb. 6:12).

7. "But thanks be to God! He gives us the victory through our Lord Jesus Christ" (1 Cor. 15:57)

71

TELEVISION

Heavenly Father, thank You that Your Word takes precedence over any other thing in my child's life. You have given him Your Word as a lamp for his feet to follow, and it lights the path he is to take in every area of his life.[1] I pray that _____ will not watch vile things or things that contradict the Word of God.[2] I pray that his own convictions will cause him to be obedient in this area because his obedience comes straight from faith.[3]

Turn _____ away from desiring any other plan but Yours, and revive his heart toward You.[4] Keep him from being like the sluggard who is too lazy to feed himself on Your Word.[5] I pray that he will not fall into useless habits concerning television but will imitate others who are walking strong with You.[6] Thank You for Your victory![7] In Jesus' name.

God's Word Says

1. "Like a city whose walls are broken down is a man who lacks self-control" (Prov. 25:28).

2. "But the fruit of the Spirit is love, joy, peace, patience, kindness, goodness, faithfulness, gentleness and self-control" (Gal. 5:22-23).

3. "It is because of him that you are in Christ Jesus, who has become for us wisdom from God — that is, our righteousness, holiness and redemption" (1 Cor. 1:30).

4. "Mockers stir up a city, but wise men turn away anger" (Prov. 29:8).

5. "A fool gives full vent to his anger, but a wise man keeps himself under control" (Prov. 29:11).

6. "If a ruler's anger rises against you, do not leave your post; calmness can lay great errors to rest" (Eccl. 10:4).

7. "But now you must rid yourselves of all such things as these: anger, rage, malice, slander, and filthy language from your lips" (Col. 3:8).

8. "Encourage the timid, help the weak, be patient with everyone. Make sure that nobody pays back wrong for wrong, but always try to be kind to each other and to everyone else" (1 Thess. 5:14-15).

72
VIOLENCE

Father, I pray that You would make my child like a fortress of self-control instead of a city whose walls are broken down.[1] Fill her with Your Spirit so she may bear Your fruit, being filled with love, joy, peace, patience, kindness, goodness, faithfulness, gentleness and self-control. No social or moral code can defy these things in her![2]

I bind the temptation of the devil in _____'s life concerning violence. Christ has been made wisdom for her,[3] and with Your help she will be a wise woman who turns away from anger.[4]

I rejoice because my child is no longer a fool giving full vent to her rage but a wise woman who keeps herself under control.[5] In her calmness she will lay great errors to rest.[6] I praise you, Father, for You are causing her to rid her life of all anger and rage,[7] replacing it with encouragement, help, patience and kindness toward others.[8] In Jesus' name.

SECTION III

RELATIONSHIPS

God's Word Says

1. "For you are a people holy to the Lord your God. The Lord your God has chosen you out of all the peoples on the face of the earth to be his people, his treasured possession" (Deut. 7:6).

2. "But you are a chosen people, a royal priesthood, a holy nation, a people belonging to God, that you may declare the praises of him who called you out of darkness into his wonderful light" (1 Pet. 2:9).

3. "No, in all these things we are more than conquerors through him who loved us" (Rom. 8:37).

4. "To the praise of the glory of his grace, by which he made us accepted in the Beloved" (Eph. 1:6, NKJV).

5. "'In the last days,' God says, 'I will pour out my Spirit on all people. Your sons and daughters will prophesy, your young men will see visions, your old men will dream dreams'" (Acts 2:17).

6. "For the Lord God is a sun and shield; the Lord bestows favor and honor; no good thing does he withhold from those whose walk is blameless" (Ps. 84:11).

7. "Do not be misled: 'Bad company corrupts good character'" (1 Cor. 15:33).

73

ACCEPTANCE

Heavenly Father, I thank You for my child's life. I thank You that he is favored by You.[1] You have called him a chosen generation, a royal priesthood and a special person.[2] Thank You for causing my child to be accepted among godly friends.

You have made _____ more than a conqueror![3] I thank You, Lord, for giving him favor and acceptance, and I ask You to allow Your acceptance to be real to him.[4] Let him know that he is wanted and needed for this end-time harvest.[5]

Father, You have promised not to withhold one good thing from my child.[6] Thank You for bringing good, godly friends across my child's path whose acceptance will help him to build good character.[7] In Jesus' name.

God's Word Says

1. "Also the hand of God was on Judah to give them singleness of heart to obey the command of the king and the leaders, at the word of the Lord" (2 Chr. 30:12, NKJV).

2. "Children, obey your parents in the Lord, for this is right. 'Honor your father and mother' — which is the first commandment with a promise — 'that it may go well with you and that you may enjoy long life on the earth'" (Eph. 6:1-3).

3. "Dear children, let us not love with words or tongue but with actions and in truth" (1 John 3:18).

4. "Blessed are the peacemakers, for they will be called sons of God. Blessed are those who are persecuted because of righteousness, for theirs is the kingdom of heaven" (Matt. 5:9-10).

5. "Although he was a son, he learned obedience from what he suffered" (Heb. 5:8).

6. "Each of you must respect his mother and father, and you must observe my Sabbaths. I am the Lord your God" (Lev. 19:3).

74
AUTHORITY

Heavenly Father, cause my child to have singleness of heart to honor and obey the people in authority over her.[1] Let her honor her father and mother so that she will have a long life, rich with Your blessings.[2]

I pray that _____ would learn to really love those in authority over her, showing her love daily by her actions.[3] As a child of God teach her to strive for peace in all areas, even when she may feel persecuted.[4]

Cause her to follow Christ's ultimate example of obedience despite adverse circumstances.[5] Let respect for those in authority over her be a part of the lifestyle she follows from this day forward.[6] In the name of Jesus.

GOD'S WORD SAYS

1. "Who redeems your life from the pit and crowns you with love and compassion" (Ps. 103:4).

2. "May the God of hope fill you with all joy and peace as you trust in him, so that you may overflow with hope by the power of the Holy Spirit" (Rom. 15:13).

3. "If one falls down, his friend can help him up. But pity the man who falls and has no one to help him up!...Though one may be overpowered, two can defend themselves. A cord of three strands is not quickly broken" (Eccl. 4:10,12).

4. "Carry each other's burdens, and in this way you will fulfill the law of Christ" (Gal. 6:2).

5. "And the second is like it: 'Love your neighbor as yourself'" (Matt. 22:39).

6. "Do not judge, and you will not be judged. Do not condemn, and you will not be condemned. Forgive, and you will be forgiven. Give, and it will be given to you. A good measure, pressed down, shaken together and running over, will be poured into your lap. For with the measure you use, it will be measured to you" (Luke 6:37-38).

7. "This is how we know what love is: Jesus Christ laid down his life for us. And we ought to lay down our lives for our brothers...Dear children, let us not love with words or tongue but with actions and in truth" (1 John 3:16,18).

75

BEARING ANOTHER'S BURDENS

Father, thank You that _____ is crowned with love and compassion[1] enabling him to reach out to others. Thank You for the power of the Holy Spirit in my child that fills him with joy and peace, and the kind of hope that naturally reaches out to those around him.[2]

I pray that when one of his friends falls down, he will help that friend up, defending his friend against the attack of the devil.[3] Let him help carry the burdens of others, thus fulfilling the law of Christ,[4] which says to "love your neighbor as yourself."[5] In so doing thank You that others will do the same for him.[6]

Thank You for Your love that teaches my child to love not only with words but by his actions as well. Teach him how to lay down his life for his friends.[7]

GOD'S WORD SAYS

1. "The wicked man flees though no one pursues, but the righteous are as bold as a lion" (Prov. 28:1).

2. "For God hath not given us the spirit of fear; but of power, and of love, and of a sound mind" (2 Tim. 1:7, KJV).

3. "For I know your eagerness to help, and I have been boasting about it to the Macedonians, telling them that since last year you in Achaia were ready to give; and your enthusiasm has stirred most of them to action" (2 Cor. 9:2).

4. "Because a great door for effective work has opened to me, and there are many who oppose me" (1 Cor. 16:9).

5. "For the Lord God is a sun and shield; the Lord bestows favor and honor; no good thing does he withhold from those whose walk is blameless" (Ps. 84:11).

6. "Now, Lord, consider their threats and enable your servants to speak your word with great boldness" (Acts 4:29).

7. "Pray also for me, that whenever I open my mouth, words may be given me so that I will fearlessly make known the mystery of the gospel, for which I am an ambassador in chains. Pray that I may declare it fearlessly, as I should" (Eph. 6:19-20).

8. "Then the disciples went out and preached everywhere, and the Lord worked with them and confirmed his word by the signs that accompanied it" (Mark 16:20).

76
BRINGING FRIENDS TO CHURCH

Heavenly Father, thank You first of all that my child has right standing with You. You said the righteous are as bold as lions![1] _____ does not hold onto fear but walks in power, love and a sound mind.[2] Her enthusiasm for going to church stirs up the others in her circle of influence.[3]

I pray that You will increase my child's circle of influence causing her to be even more effective with her witness.[4] Give her favor and honor with her friends[5] so that they will be responsive to her invitations. Enable her to speak with great boldness,[6] fearlessly making known the mystery of the gospel.[7]

Thank You that You are working with her as she invites her friends to church. You are already working in their hearts, giving them a desire to know You more intently.[8] In Jesus' name.

GOD'S WORD SAYS

1. "All your sons will be taught by the Lord, and great will be your children's peace" (Is. 54:13).

2. "To be made new in the attitude of your minds; and to put on the new self, created to be like God in true righteousness and holiness" (Eph. 4:23-24).

3. "Let the wise listen and add to their learning, and let the discerning get guidance" (Prov. 1:5).

4. "Finally, brothers, good-by. Aim for perfection, listen to my appeal, be of one mind, live in peace. And the God of love and peace will be with you" (2 Cor. 13:11).

5. "My dear brothers, take note of this: Everyone should be quick to listen, slow to speak and slow to become angry" (James 1:19).

77

COMMUNICATION

Heavenly Father, thank You that _____ is being taught by Your Spirit and is governed by Your peace.[1] Thank You for giving him a new attitude of mind which produces righteousness and holiness in his life.[2]

Cause him to pay attention and learn more about effective communication with our family and others. Increase his discernment so that he will be divinely guided in every action.[3] Give him a desire to perfect his communication skills so that he will be a good listener, be of one mind in every communication and live in peace with others.[4] Help him to be quick to listen, slow to speak and slow to become angry.[5] In Jesus' name!

GOD'S WORD SAYS

1. "For God did not give us a spirit of timidity, but a spirit of power, of love and of self-discipline" (2 Tim. 1:7).

2. "How good and pleasant it is when brothers live together in unity!" (Ps. 133:1).

3. "Salt is good, but if it loses its saltiness, how can you make it salty again? Have salt in yourselves, and be at peace with each other" (Mark 9:50).

4. "Accept one another, then, just as Christ accepted you, in order to bring praise to God" (Rom. 15:7).

5. "Make every effort to live in peace with all men and to be holy; without holiness no one will see the Lord" (Heb. 12:14).

78
CONFLICT

Heavenly Father, I thank You for giving my child a spirit of power, love and self-discipline.[1] I know it is Your will that she live peaceably among her friends. It is good and pleasant in Your sight to live in unity and peace with one another.[2] I pray that _____ will not forsake the power of the gospel by living in strife but will let the preserving effect of Your Holy Spirit work within her.[3]

I thank You for helping my child to resolve conflict in her life by working in her to accept others just as You have accepted her.[4] Help my child to put forth the effort it takes to live in peace with all people.[5] In Jesus' name.

GOD'S WORD SAYS

1. "For we know that our old self was crucified with him so that the body of sin might be done away with, that we should no longer be slaves to sin" (Rom. 6:6).

2. "For we do not have a high priest who is unable to sympathize with our weaknesses, but we have one who has been tempted in every way, just as we are — yet was without sin. Let us then approach the throne of grace with confidence, so that we may receive mercy and find grace to help us in our time of need" (Heb. 4:15-16).

3. "Rather, clothe yourselves with the Lord Jesus Christ, and do not think about how to gratify the desires of the sinful nature" (Rom. 13:14).

4. "Those who belong to Christ Jesus have crucified the sinful nature with its passions and desires" (Gal. 5:24).

5. "Do not conform any longer to the pattern of this world, but be transformed by the renewing of your mind. Then you will be able to test and approve what God's will is — his good, pleasing and perfect will" (Rom. 12:2).

6. "We demolish arguments and every pretension that sets itself up against the knowledge of God, and we take captive every thought to make it obedient to Christ" (2 Cor. 10:5).

7. "Finally, brothers, whatever is true, whatever is noble, whatever is right, whatever is pure, whatever is lovely, whatever is admirable — if anything is excellent or praiseworthy — think about such things" (Phil. 4:8).

79

CONTROLLING SEXUAL DESIRES

Heavenly Father, thank You that my child's sinful desires were nailed to the cross with Jesus. The part of him that loves to sin was crushed and fatally wounded. His body is no longer under sin's control, and he no longer needs to be a slave to sin.[1] Thank You for the help that Jesus provides to resist temptation[2] so that he won't even want to make plans to gratify sinful desires.[3] I glorify Your holy name for nailing my child's sinful and fleshly cravings to the cross where they are crucified.[4]

Thank You, Father, for renewing _____'s mind through Your Word.[5] May he allow You to capture his imagination and thoughts, bringing his mind into obedience to Christ![6] Fix his thoughts on things that are true, noble, right, pure, lovely, admirable, excellent and praiseworthy.[7] In Jesus' name.

GOD'S WORD SAYS

1. "For it is God who works in you to will and to act according to his good purpose" (Phil. 2:13).

2. "Listen, my son, accept what I say, and the years of your life will be many" (Prov. 4:10).

3. "Come to me, all you who are weary and burdened, and I will give you rest" (Matt. 11:28).

4. "Do you not know that your body is a temple of the Holy Spirit, who is in you, whom you have received from God? You are not your own" (1 Cor. 6:19).

5. "At this I awoke and looked around. My sleep had been pleasant to me" (Jer. 31:26).

80
CURFEWS

Heavenly Father, thank You for working with the desires inside of my child so she can follow Your will and act as You want her to.[1] I pray that _____ would not push the limits of my authority when it comes to curfews but that she will honor them and live a blessed life.[2] Show her that as she is faithful in this she will be given more responsibility.

I pray that my child would strive to maintain godly rest in her life[3] and not be unwise in staying out as late as possible. Holy Spirit, remind her to take care of her physical body because it is Your temple.[4] Thank You, Lord, for giving my child refreshing and pleasant sleep[5] because she honors You in her life.

GOD'S WORD SAYS

1. "But now I am writing you that you must not associate with anyone who calls himself a brother but is sexually immoral or greedy, an idolater or a slanderer, a drunkard or a swindler. With such a man do not even eat" (1 Cor. 5:11).

2. "A righteous man is cautious in friendship, but the way of the wicked leads them astray" (Prov. 12:26).

3. "Do not be yoked together with unbelievers. For what do righteousness and wickedness have in common? Or what fellowship can light have with darkness?" (2 Cor. 6:14).

4. "Flee the evil desires of youth, and pursue righteousness, faith, love and peace, along with those who call on the Lord out of a pure heart" (2 Tim. 2:22).

5. "Do not make friends with a hot-tempered man, do not associate with one easily angered" (Prov. 22:24).

6. "Do nothing out of selfish ambition or vain conceit, but in humility consider others better than yourselves. Each of you should look not only to your own interests, but also to the interests of others" (Phil. 2:3-4).

7. "May the God who gives endurance and encouragement give you a spirit of unity among yourselves as you follow Christ Jesus" (Rom. 15:5).

81

DATING STANDARDS

Heavenly Father, show my child the kind of person You desire for him to date. May he not keep company with anyone who claims to be a Christian but indulges in sexual sins or in greed, idolatry, drunkenness or abuse.[1] Let him choose his friends carefully.[2]

Cause _____ to remember that he is clothed with the righteousness of Christ and has nothing in common with the wickedness of sinful people.[3] Let him run from ungodly desires, enjoying only the companionship of others who pursue righteousness, faith, love, peace and purity of heart.[4]

Thank You that my child avoids angry, short-tempered people.[5] Give him an unselfish, modest, humble attitude that puts others first.[6] May all his dating relationships be filled with patience, encouragement and an attitude of unity.[7] In Jesus' name.

GOD'S WORD SAYS

1. "Fathers, do not exasperate your children; instead, bring them up in the training and instruction of the Lord" (Eph. 6:4).

2. "Not that I have already obtained all this, or have already been made perfect, but I press on to take hold of that for which Christ Jesus took hold of me" (Phil. 3:12).

3. "For acquiring a disciplined and prudent life, doing what is right and just and fair" (Prov. 1:3).

4. "Train a child in the way he should go, and when he is old he will not turn from it" (Prov. 22:6).

5. "Because the Lord disciplines those he loves, as a father the son he delights in" (Prov. 3:12).

6. "He will die for lack of discipline, led astray by his own great folly" (Prov. 5:23).

7. "For these commands are a lamp, this teaching is a light, and the corrections of discipline are the way to life" (Prov. 6:23).

8. "The thief comes only to steal and kill and destroy; I have come that they may have life, and have it to the full" (John 10:10).

82
DISCIPLINE

Heavenly Father, I praise You for showing me how to bring my child up with training and instruction from You.[1] Help me to show her the path and direction You have prepared for her life so that she may take hold of Your eternal destiny.[2]

Thank You for sending Your Word to help her acquire a divine purpose for her life which produces a disciplined lifestyle.[3] I pray that _____ will understand the need for discipline in her own life and that she would not depart from the training and discipline she is learning in our home.[4]

You delight in _____, and use the discipline in our home as a way to show Your love to her.[5] In the name of Jesus, my child will not be led away by foolishness or die spiritually for lack of discipline.[6] Thank You that discipline is the way to life.[7] Give my child abundant life — life to its fullness.[8]

God's Word Says

1. "For surely, O Lord, you bless the righteous; you surround them with your favor as with a shield" (Ps. 5:12).

2. "Be devoted to one another in brotherly love. Honor one another above yourselves" (Rom. 12:10).

3. "It [love] is not rude, it is not self-seeking, it is not easily angered, it keeps no record of wrongs" (1 Cor. 13:5).

4. "A man of many companions may come to ruin, but there is a friend who sticks closer than a brother" (Prov. 18:24).

5. "And hope does not disappoint us, because God has poured out his love into our hearts by the Holy Spirit, whom he has given us" (Rom. 5:5).

6. "Our help is in the name of the Lord, the Maker of heaven and earth" (Ps. 124:8).

7. "But the Lord is righteous; he has cut me free from the cords of the wicked" (Ps. 129:4).

8. "Even my close friend, whom I trusted, he who shared my bread, has lifted up his heel against me. But you, O Lord, have mercy on me; raise me up, that I may repay them. I know that you are pleased with me, for my enemy does not triumph over me" (Ps. 41:9-11).

9. "But I tell you: Love your enemies and pray for those who persecute you" (Matt. 5:44).

83

DISLOYALTY FROM FRIENDS

Heavenly Father, thank You for surrounding my child with a shield of favor so that he makes friends easily.[1] I pray that You will keep him devoted to his friends in brotherly love, honoring others above himself.[2]

Keep him from offense even when others wrong him.[3] Help him to realize that even though some people just pretend to be friends, You are the One who sticks closer than a brother.[4] His security lies in You, for You are the One who helps him. You are the glory and the lifter of his head, pouring Your love into his heart.[5]

When _____ 's friends are disloyal to him, You will be his help,[6] for You have cut him free from the cords of deceitful men.[7] Thank You for Your mercy and strength which raises him up when close, trusted friends seem to reject his friendship. You will be pleased with my child, and his enemies will not triumph or get the best of him.[8] Remind him to love his enemies and pray for those who persecute him.[9] In Jesus' name.

GOD'S WORD SAYS

1. "If it is encouraging, let him encourage; if it is contributing to the needs of others, let him give generously; if it is leadership, let him govern diligently; if it is showing mercy, let him do it cheerfully" (Rom. 12:8).

2. "For God's gifts and his call are irrevocable" (Rom. 11:29).

3. "Therefore encourage one another and build each other up, just as in fact you are doing" (1 Thess. 5:11).

4. "A generous man will prosper; he who refreshes others will himself be refreshed" (Prov. 11:25).

5. "And we urge you, brothers, warn those who are idle, encourage the timid, help the weak, be patient with everyone. Make sure that nobody pays back wrong for wrong, but always try to be kind to each other and to everyone else" (1 Thess. 5:14-15).

6. "May our Lord Jesus Christ himself and God our Father, who loved us and by his grace gave us eternal encouragement and good hope" (2 Thess. 2:16).

7. "He must hold firmly to the trustworthy message as it has been taught, so that he can encourage others by sound doctrine and refute those who oppose it" (Titus 1:9).

84
ENCOURAGING OTHERS

Thank You, heavenly Father, for moving on my child to become more of an encourager every day. I pray that the gift of encouragement[1] will increase in _____ 's life, for Your gifts and Your call are irrevocable.[2]

I pray that she will encourage others always and build them up.[3] For as she is building up others, she will be built up![4] Even the timid and the weak will be inspired by my child's kindness and patience.[5]

Thank You, Father, for the eternal encouragement and good hope that _____ has in You. Strengthen her every considerate act and word toward others.[6] Thank You that she will encourage others with her sound and solid beliefs.[7] In Jesus' name.

GOD'S WORD SAYS

1. "Those who live according to the sinful nature have their minds set on what that nature desires; but those who live in accordance with the Spirit have their minds set on what the Spirit desires" (Rom. 8:5).

2. "For this reason, since the day we heard about you, we have not stopped praying for you and asking God to fill you with the knowledge of his will through all spiritual wisdom and understanding. And we pray this in order that you may live a life worthy of the Lord and may please him in every way: bearing fruit in every good work, growing in the knowledge of God, being strengthened with all power according to his glorious might so that you may have great endurance and patience, and joyfully giving thanks to the Father, who has qualified you to share in the inheritance of the saints in the kingdom of light" (Col. 1:9-12).

3. "Therefore, I urge you, brothers, in view of God's mercy, to offer your bodies as living sacrifices, holy and pleasing to God — this is your spiritual act of worship" (Rom. 12:1).

4. "Then make my joy complete by being like-minded, having the same love, being one in spirit and purpose" (Phil. 2:2).

85
EXPRESSING AFFECTION

Heavenly Father, thank You that _____ lives in accordance with Your Holy Spirit, having his mind set on what Your Spirit desires.[1] I pray the affection he expresses in his dating relationships will enable his friend to live a life worthy of the Lord so that both he and she will please the Lord by their actions. May their relationship bear spiritual fruit as they are strengthened by God's power, qualified to share in the inheritance of God.[2]

I pray that _____ will present his body and its affectionate expressions as a living sacrifice to You, holy and pleasing to God as an act of spiritual worship.[3] I pray that each of his dating relationships will display godly qualities of love for You and unity of spirit and purpose.[4] In Jesus' name.

God's Word Says

1. "But the wisdom that comes from heaven is first of all pure; then peace-loving, considerate, submissive, full of mercy and good fruit, impartial and sincere" (James 3:17).

2. "So give your servant a discerning heart to govern your people and to distinguish between right and wrong. For who is able to govern this great people of yours?" (1 Kin. 3:9).

3. "The Lord will guide you always; he will satisfy your needs in a sun-scorched land and will strengthen your frame. You will be like a well-watered garden, like a spring whose waters never fail" (Is. 58:11).

4. "Because you know that the testing of your faith develops perseverance. Perseverance must finish its work so that you may be mature and complete, not lacking anything" (James 1:3-4).

5. "In the same way, the Spirit helps us in our weakness. We do not know what we ought to pray for, but the Spirit himself intercedes for us with groans that words cannot express. And he who searches our hearts knows the mind of the Spirit, because the Spirit intercedes for the saints in accordance with God's will" (Rom. 8:26-27).

6. "He who finds a wife finds what is good and receives favor from the Lord" (Prov. 18:22).

86

FINDING A MARRIAGE PARTNER

Heavenly Father, thank You for giving my child wisdom that is pure, peace-loving, considerate, submissive, full of mercy and good fruit, impartial and sincere.[1] May these characteristics shine forth in her life and in the life of her future mate. Help her to have an understanding heart, discerning between good and evil in people's character.[2]

Thank You for guiding _____ continually in her preparation for a spouse. Let her be like a well-watered garden, like an ever-flowing spring![3] Allow the testing of her faith to produce perseverance so that she can be mature and complete, lacking nothing.[4]

Father, assure my child of the Holy Spirit's help in her weaknesses, even the groanings uttered on her behalf. Search her heart that she may know the mind of the Spirit who intercedes according to Your will concerning marriage.[5] Thank You that You are looking after her and that she will find a good spouse and obtain blessings and favor from You.[6]

God's Word Says

1. "Be devoted to one another in brotherly love. Honor one another above yourselves" (Rom. 12:10).

2. "For if you forgive men when they sin against you, your heavenly Father will also forgive you" (Matt. 6:14).

3. "Be kind and compassionate to one another, forgiving each other, just as in Christ God forgave you" (Eph. 4:32).

4. "Be self-controlled and alert. Your enemy the devil prowls around like a roaring lion looking for someone to devour. Resist him, standing firm in the faith, because you know that your brothers throughout the world are undergoing the same kind of sufferings" (1 Pet. 5:8-9).

5. "Do not repay evil with evil or insult with insult, but with blessing, because to this you were called so that you may inherit a blessing" (1 Pet. 3:9).

6. "If we confess our sins, he is faithful and just and will forgive us our sins and purify us from all unrighteousness" (1 John 1:9).

7. "Be imitators of God, therefore, as dearly loved children" (Eph. 5:1).

87

FORGIVENESS

Heavenly Father, I pray that my child would be devoted to his family members in brotherly love and put others above himself.[1] Help him to walk in forgiveness toward others as You cause him to remember how You have forgiven him of his sins.[2]

Cause _____ to be kind and tenderhearted toward others, even if he may have been wronged.[3] I rebuke every attitude of revenge and vindictiveness that would try to destroy my family, and I pray that You would keep my child from snapping at others.[4] Instead prompt him to pray for Your help and power to fill those who may offend him, and bless him for his kindness.[5]

Cause Your forgiveness to be real to my child, let him encounter Your faithfulness and justice.[6] Let him follow the example of Christ by being full of love for others.[7] In Jesus' name.

God's Word Says

1. "Cast all your anxiety on him because he cares for you" (1 Pet. 5:7).

2. "Love is patient, love is kind. It does not envy, it does not boast, it is not proud. It is not rude, it is not self-seeking, it is not easily angered, it keeps no record of wrongs. Love does not delight in evil but rejoices with the truth. It always protects, always trusts, always hopes, always perseveres. Love never fails. But where there are prophecies, they will cease; where there are tongues, they will be stilled; where there is knowledge, it will pass away" (1 Cor. 13:4-8).

3. "Above all else, guard your heart, for it is the wellspring of life" (Prov. 4:23).

4. "Because your heart was responsive and you humbled yourself before God when you heard what he spoke against this place and its people, and because you humbled yourself before me and tore your robes and wept in my presence, I have heard you, declares the Lord" (2 Chr. 34:27).

5. "Instead, it should be that of your inner self, the unfading beauty of a gentle and quiet spirit, which is of great worth in God's sight" (1 Pet. 3:4).

6. "For it is God who works in you to will and to act according to his good purpose" (Phil. 2:13).

88
FUTURE SPOUSE

Heavenly Father, I lift up my daughter's future spouse before You. You lovingly care about every detail of his life.[1] Thank You for preparing him in Your kind of love. In Jesus' name he is patient, kind, never envious, boastful or proud. He is not rude, self-seeking, easily angered or quick to keep record of wrongs. He does not delight in evil but rejoices in the truth. He always protects, trusts, hopes and perseveres. Your love causes him to be victorious every time![2] I ask that You will guard and protect his heart from offenses that may come his way.[3] Keep his heart tender and responsive before You.[4]

Thank You for making him a beautiful person in his heart with the lasting appeal of a gentle and quiet spirit which is so precious to You![5] You are at work in him even now to will and to act according to the good purposes You have for him and my daughter as a married couple.[6] In Jesus' name.

GOD'S WORD SAYS

1. "A gossip betrays a confidence, but a trustworthy man keeps a secret" (Prov. 11:13).

2. "Without wood a fire goes out; without gossip a quarrel dies down" (Prov. 26:20).

3. "May the words of my mouth and the meditation of my heart be pleasing in your sight, O Lord, my Rock and my Redeemer" (Ps. 19:14).

4. "Do not let any unwholesome talk come out of your mouths, but only what is helpful for building others up according to their needs, that it may benefit those who listen" (Eph. 4:29).

5. "Nor should there be obscenity, foolish talk or coarse joking, which are out of place, but rather thanksgiving" (Eph. 5:4).

6. "Avoid godless chatter, because those who indulge in it will become more and more ungodly" (2 Tim. 2:16).

7. "With the tongue we praise our Lord and Father, and with it we curse men, who have been made in God's likeness" (James 3:9).

89
GOSSIPING

Heavenly Father, I pray that You will keep my child trustworthy guarding any confidence he has with others, not like a gossip who betrays.[1] I pray that _____ will learn to stay out of other people's quarrels so as not to add wood to the fire.[2] May the words of his mouth and the meditations of his heart be pleasing in Your sight.[3]

I pray that my child will not let unwholesome talk come out of his mouth but will say only what is helpful for building others up according to their needs. Cause his words to be a benefit to everyone who listens.[4]
Thank You that he replaces foolish talk with thanksgiving.[5] Help him to avoid godless chatter, whether it be in speaking or in listening.[6] Let his mouth be used for praising God and building up others only![7]
In Jesus' name.

GOD'S WORD SAYS

1. "No, in all these things we are more than conquerors through him who loved us" (Rom. 8:37).

2. "Let us not become conceited, provoking and envying each other" (Gal. 5:26).

3. "Love is patient, love is kind. It does not envy, it does not boast, it is not proud" (1 Cor. 13:4).

4. "May integrity and uprightness protect me, because my hope is in you" (Ps. 25:21).

5. "We demolish arguments and every pretension that sets itself up against the knowledge of God, and we take captive every thought to make it obedient to Christ" (2 Cor. 10:5).

6. "Rather, clothe yourselves with the Lord Jesus Christ, and do not think about how to gratify the desires of the sinful nature" (Rom. 13:14).

7. "Rejoice with those who rejoice; mourn with those who mourn" (Rom. 12:15-16).

90
HANDLING JEALOUSY

Heavenly Father, I pray that through Christ's love my child is more than a conqueror over jealousy in her relationships.[1] Keep her from being puffed up with pride or becoming conceited so that she will be able to avoid every bit of envy and jealousy.[2] Release Your love in _____; love that is never jealous, envious, boastful or proud.[3]

Protect her from jealousy with integrity and character. Cause her to set her hope on You first and foremost.[4] Father, move on her to take authority over every jealous thought bringing them captive into the obedience of Christ.[5] May she clothe herself with Christ, not thinking about the gratification of her sinful nature through jealousy.[6] May she rejoice with those who rejoice and weep with those who weep, living in harmony with others.[7] In Jesus' name.

God's Word Says

1. "Keep your lives free from the love of money and be content with what you have, because God has said, 'Never will I leave you; never will I forsake you'" (Heb. 13:5).

2. "Since you are precious and honored in my sight, and because I love you, I will give men in exchange for you, and people in exchange for your life" (Is. 43:4).

3. "He lifted me out of the slimy pit, out of the mud and mire; he set my feet on a rock and gave me a firm place to stand. He put a new song in my mouth, a hymn of praise to our God. Many will see and fear and put their trust in the Lord" (Ps. 40:2-3).

4. "The Lord is close to the brokenhearted and saves those who are crushed in spirit" (Ps. 34:18)

5. "And the peace of God, which transcends all understanding, will guard your hearts and your minds in Christ Jesus" (Phil. 4:7).

6. "This then is how we know that we belong to the truth, and how we set our hearts at rest in his presence whenever our hearts condemn us. For God is greater than our hearts, and he knows everything" (1 John 3:19-20).

7. "My flesh and my heart may fail, but God is the strength of my heart and my portion forever" (Ps. 73:26).

91
HEALING A BROKEN HEART

Heavenly Father, thank You that You never leave us or forsake us.[1] May my child comprehend how precious and honored he is to You, recognizing how much You love him.[2] Even though he may feel as though others have let him down, wrap Your arms of comfort around him at this time assuring him that You are his rock, putting a new song of joy in his heart because of Your faithfulness.[3]

Thank You, Father, that You have promised to be near to those who have a broken heart.[4] Wrap _____ in Your peace that surpasses all understanding and guard his heart and mind in Christ.[5] Even when my child's own heart condemns him, set it at rest in Your presence. You are greater than his heart, Lord, and You have a much greater understanding of the whole situation![6] I praise You for being the strength of his heart and his portion forever.[7] In Jesus' name.

God's Word Says

1. "Children, obey your parents in the Lord, for this is right. 'Honor your father and mother' — which is the first commandment with a promise — 'that it may go well with you and that you may enjoy long life on the earth'" (Eph. 6:1-3).

2. "Remind the people to be subject to rulers and authorities, to be obedient, to be ready to do whatever is good" (Titus 3:1).

3. "Since you know that you will receive an inheritance from the Lord as a reward. It is the Lord Christ you are serving" (Col. 3:24).

4. "Do everything without complaining or arguing, so that you may become blameless and pure, children of God without fault in a crooked and depraved generation, in which you shine like stars in the universe" (Phil. 2:14-15).

5. "May the words of my mouth and the meditation of my heart be pleasing in your sight, O Lord, my Rock and my Redeemer" (Ps. 19:14).

6. "Let your gentleness be evident to all. The Lord is near" (Phil. 4:5).

7. "Dear children, let us not love with words or tongue but with actions and in truth" (1 John 3:18)

92
HONOR

Heavenly Father, give my child a heart that wants not only to obey us as her parents but one that honors us as well. I thank You for pouring out a huge blessing on her life because of it.[1]

Cause _____ to be obedient, eager and willing to do whatever is right.[2] Help her to work hard and cheerfully at everything she does just as though she were working for You.[3] Give her the attitude of a servant who does everything without complaining or arguing, making her blameless and pure in the midst of a crooked and perverse generation.[4]

May the words of my child's mouth, as well as the thoughts she dwells upon, be pleasing in Your sight.[5] I pray that You will make my child unselfish and considerate around our home and with every member of her family.[6] Thank You for enabling Your love to shine through her life, which results in her loving others not only in words but with actions and pure motives.[7] In Jesus' name.

God's Word Says

1. "Children, obey your parents in the Lord, for this is right" (Eph. 6:1).

2. "Train a child in the way he should go, and when he is old he will not turn from it" (Prov. 22:6).

3. "Not only so, but we also rejoice in our sufferings, because we know that suffering produces perseverance; perseverance, character; and character, hope" (Rom. 5:3-4).

4. "I have been crucified with Christ and I no longer live, but Christ lives in me. The life I live in the body, I live by faith in the Son of God, who loved me and gave himself for me" (Gal. 2:20).

93
HOUSEHOLD RULES

Heavenly Father, thank You for helping my child to be obedient to our rules, for this is the right thing to do.[1] You said if we train up our child in the way he should go, when he is old he will not depart from it.[2] Thank You that the rules we have established in our home will be effective in training our son to be obedient and disciplined.

I praise You, Lord, for giving my child perseverance to respect the rules, even when he may not want to, so that his character may become solid and unshakable. That character will produce hope in him, and that hope will not disappoint him.[3] I pray that You will help him learn to crucify himself with Christ so Christ will live in him, making it possible for _____ to respect and honor the rules and authority of this home.[4] Thank You for blessing and encouraging him with Your Spirit, for spurring him to excellence and for equipping him for the future that You have for him. In Jesus' name.

GOD'S WORD SAYS

1. "And lead us not into temptation, but deliver us from the evil one" (Matt. 6:13).

2. "For he has rescued us from the dominion of darkness and brought us into the kingdom of the Son he loves" (Col. 1:13).

3. "The night is nearly over; the day is almost here. So let us put aside the deeds of darkness and put on the armor of light. Let us behave decently, as in the daytime, not in orgies and drunkenness, not in sexual immorality and debauchery, not in dissension and jealousy" (Rom. 13:12-13).

4. "Finally, be strong in the Lord and in his mighty power" (Eph. 6:10).

5. "Have you not put a hedge around him and his household and everything he has? You have blessed the work of his hands, so that his flocks and herds are spread throughout the land" (Job 1:10).

6. "For certain men whose condemnation was written about long ago have secretly slipped in among you. They are godless men, who change the grace of our God into a license for immorality and deny Jesus Christ our only Sovereign and Lord" (Jude 4).

7. "It is God's will that you should be sanctified: that you should avoid sexual immorality" (1 Thess. 4:3).

8. "Put to death, therefore, whatever belongs to your earthly nature: sexual immorality, impurity, lust, evil desires and greed, which is idolatry" (Col. 3:5).

9. "So if the Son sets you free, you will be free indeed" (John 8:36).

94

IMMORALITY

I praise You, heavenly Father, for Your delivering power over temptation.[1] Thank You for translating my child out of darkness into the kingdom of light.[2] You are her armor of light, enabling her to behave decently, shrugging off immorality of any kind in her relationships.[3] Father, I ask You to keep my child strong in You.[4]

I pray a hedge of protection around _____, asking Your protection from every person, place or thing that would try to destroy her.[5] May she sense Your grace surrounding her but never use that grace as license for immorality, thereby denying Jesus.[6] Let her follow Your will in sanctification.[7] I pray that she would put to death everything that belongs to her earthly nature, including sexual immorality, impurity, lust, evil desires and greed.[8]

I praise You because my child walks free in the liberty You purchased for her.[9] In Jesus' name.

GOD'S WORD SAYS

1. "I led them with cords of human kindness, with ties of love; I lifted the yoke from their neck and bent down to feed them" (Hos. 11:4).

2. "In purity, understanding, patience and kindness; in the Holy Spirit and in sincere love" (2 Cor. 6:6).

3. "Therefore, as God's chosen people, holy and dearly loved, clothe yourselves with compassion, kindness, humility, gentleness and patience" (Col. 3:12).

4. "But the fruit of the Spirit is love, joy, peace, patience, kindness, goodness, faithfulness, gentleness and self-control" (Gal. 5:22-23).

5. "Or do you show contempt for the riches of his kindness, tolerance and patience, not realizing that God's kindness leads you toward repentance?" (Rom. 2:4).

6. "He saved us, not because of righteous things we had done, but because of his mercy. He saved us through the washing of rebirth and renewal by the Holy Spirit" (Titus 3:5).

7. "Make every effort to add to your faith goodness; and to goodness, knowledge; and to knowledge, self-control; and to self-control, perseverance; and to perseverance, godliness; and to godliness, brotherly kindness; and to brotherly kindness, love" (2 Pet. 1:5-7).

8. "If we are being called to account today for an act of kindness shown to a cripple and are asked how he was healed" (Acts 4:9).

95

KINDNESS

Thank You, Father, for leading my child with cords of kindness and ties of love.[1] I ask that he remain patient and kind toward everyone, walking in Your Spirit and expressing sincere love.[2] May he clothe himself with compassion, kindness, gentleness and humility.[3] Your Spirit within him will produce the fruit of kindness.[4]

Thank You for Your ultimate example of kindness which leads all men to repentance.[5] Cause that kindness to appear to _____ daily, reminding him that his salvation is not the result of his own goodness but Your gift of kindness.[6] I pray that my child's faith in You will be strengthened as a result of exercising brotherly love at all times.[7] May his acts of kindness cause people's lives around him to be healed.[8] In Jesus' name.

GOD'S WORD SAYS

1. "Whoever does not love does not know God, because God is love" (1 John 4:8).

2. "And to know this love that surpasses knowledge — that you may be filled to the measure of all the fullness of God" (Eph. 3:19).

3. "A new command I give you: Love one another. As I have loved you, so you must love one another. By this all men will know that you are my disciples, if you love one another" (John 13:34-35).

4. "Be devoted to one another in brotherly love. Honor one another above yourselves" (Rom. 12:10).

5. "Let no debt remain outstanding, except the continuing debt to love one another, for he who loves his fellowman has fulfilled the law" (Rom. 13:8).

6. "You, my brothers, were called to be free. But do not use your freedom to indulge the sinful nature; rather, serve one another in love" (Gal. 5:13).

7. "Be completely humble and gentle; be patient, bearing with one another in love" (Eph. 4:2).

8. "And hope does not disappoint us, because God has poured out his love into our hearts by the Holy Spirit, whom he has given us" (Rom. 5:5).

9. "And let us consider how we may spur one another on toward love and good deeds" (Heb. 10:24).

96
LOVING ONE ANOTHER

Heavenly Father, Your Word tells us that to truly love one another we have to know the love that You have for us, for You are love![1] I pray that You will flood my child's heart with the revelation of Your love; that she will experience it and know it like never before,[2] enabling her to love others as You love her. Then her friends will know she is Your disciple.[3] I pray that she will be devoted to others, putting them above herself.[4]

Thank You that _____ fulfills Your law by continuing to love the unlovable.[5] May she never use the freedom You gave her to indulge in her sinful nature but to serve others freely with a pure heart.[6] I pray she will bear with others, being patient and showing love.[7]

Father, I praise You for the love of Christ which You poured into my child through Your Holy Spirit.[8] I pray it will help her spur others to love and to do good works.[9] In Jesus' name.

GOD'S WORD SAYS

1. "Blessed is the man who does not walk in the counsel of the wicked or stand in the way of sinners or sit in the seat of mockers. But his delight is in the law of the Lord, and on his law he meditates day and night. He is like a tree planted by streams of water, which yields its fruit in season and whose leaf does not wither. Whatever he does prospers" (Ps. 1:1-3).

2. "It is because of him that you are in Christ Jesus, who has become for us wisdom from God — that is, our righteousness, holiness and redemption" (1 Cor. 1:30).

3. "He who walks with the wise grows wise, but a companion of fools suffers harm" (Prov. 13:20).

4. "Flee the evil desires of youth, and pursue righteousness, faith, love and peace, along with those who call on the Lord out of a pure heart" (2 Tim. 2:22).

5. "Thus you will walk in the ways of good men and keep to the paths of the righteous" (Prov. 2:20).

97
MAKING GODLY FRIENDS

Heavenly Father, bring godly friends into my child's life. Help him to avoid the advice, counsel and fellowship of sinners. May he be like a tree planted by streams of water, yielding good fruit and delighting in Your way and plan concerning friendships.[1]

Thank You for Jesus who became wisdom for my child.[2] Enable him to grow with his friends in the wisdom of Christ.[3] Let _____ be a friend to all who fear You and follow Your ways.

Thank You that my child will not be alone and easily overpowered but will possess godly friendships that will be his defense against the enemy. I pray You will keep him in pursuit of what is right; that he will enjoy the companionship of those who love You with a pure heart.[4] In Jesus' name thank You for letting my child walk in the ways of good men and keep to the paths of the righteous.[5]

God's Word Says

1. "And hope does not disappoint us, because God has poured out his love into our hearts by the Holy Spirit, whom he has given us" (Rom. 5:5).

2. "It is not rude, it is not self-seeking, it is not easily angered, it keeps no record of wrongs...It always protects, always trusts, always hopes, always perseveres" (1 Cor. 13:5,7).

3. "I am your servant; give me discernment that I may understand your statutes" (Ps. 119:125).

4. "My son, preserve sound judgment and discernment, do not let them out of your sight" (Prov. 3:21).

5. "It is not good to have zeal without knowledge, nor to be hasty and miss the way" (Prov. 19:2).

6. "You will increase my honor and comfort me once again" (Ps. 71:21).

7. "Not only so, but we also rejoice in our sufferings, because we know that suffering produces perseverance; perseverance, character; and character, hope. And hope does not disappoint us, because God has poured out his love into our hearts by the Holy Spirit, whom he has given us" (Rom. 5:3-5).

98
Misunderstandings

Heavenly Father, thank You for Your love which is shed abroad in my child's heart.[1] That love makes her slow to anger, willing to believe the best of other people and ready to avoid misunderstandings.[2] Thank You for giving her discernment.[3] I pray that _____ will have sound judgment in every situation.[4] Keep my child from being hasty or jumping to conclusions so that she does not damage her relationships with her family and friends.[5]

Comfort her and increase her understanding so that she will not become a victim of misunderstandings.[6] Father, help her rejoice in the midst of sufferings which produce perseverance, character and hope in You. That way she'll never be disappointed![7] In Jesus' name.

God's Word Says

1. "Through him and for his name's sake, we received grace and apostleship to call people from among all the Gentiles to the obedience that comes from faith" (Rom. 1:5).

2. "Consequently, he who rebels against the authority is rebelling against what God has instituted, and those who do so will bring judgment on themselves" (Rom. 13:2).

3. "All these blessings will come upon you and accompany you if you obey the Lord your God: You will be blessed in the city and blessed in the country. The fruit of your womb will be blessed, and the crops of your land and the young of your livestock— the calves of your herds and the lambs of your flocks. Your basket and your kneading trough will be blessed. You will be blessed when you come in and blessed when you go out. The Lord will grant that the enemies who rise up against you will be defeated before you. They will come at you from one direction but flee from you in seven. The Lord will send a blessing on your barns and on everything you put your hand to. The Lord your God will bless you in the land he is giving you" (Deut. 28:2-8).

4. "Children, obey your parents in the Lord [as His representatives], for this is just and right. Honor (esteem and value as precious) your father and your mother — this is the first commandment with a promise — [Ex. 20:12]. That all may be well with you and that you may live long on the earth" (Eph. 6:1-3, AMP).

99
OBEDIENCE

Dear heavenly Father, I pray that my child will walk in godly obedience, obeying Your plan because of his faith.[1] Cause him to see that when he disobeys the rules of our home, he is choosing to bring judgment upon himself.[2]

I praise You for clearly stating the blessings for those who obey You. Thank You that as long as _____ chooses to be obedient he will be blessed no matter where life takes him. Even his children will be blessed because of the obedience he practices, and he will never be in want. Before he goes somewhere and after he leaves, You will bless him continually. There will be a lifelong blessing upon his storehouse and upon the work of his hands.[3]

I thank You that my child will not scorn obedience but will honor us as his parents, esteeming and valuing us as precious — those who are in authority over him causing all to go well with him and his future.[4] In Jesus' name.

God's Word Says

1. "The Spirit of the Lord is on me, because he has anointed me to preach good news to the poor. He has sent me to proclaim freedom for the prisoners and recovery of sight for the blind, to release the oppressed" (Luke 4:18).

2. "And hope does not disappoint us, because God has poured out his love into our hearts by the Holy Spirit, whom he has given us" (Rom. 5:5).

3. "He who covers over an offense promotes love, but whoever repeats the matter separates close friends" (Prov. 17:9).

4. "Love is patient, love is kind. It does not envy, it does not boast, it is not proud. It is not rude, it is not self-seeking, it is not easily angered, it keeps no record of wrongs" (1 Cor. 13:4-5).

5. "But the wisdom that comes from heaven is first of all pure; then peace-loving, considerate, submissive, full of mercy and good fruit, impartial and sincere" (James 3:17).

6. "A man's wisdom gives him patience; it is to his glory to overlook an offense" (Prov. 19:11).

7. "Be kind and compassionate to one another, forgiving each other, just as in Christ God forgave you" (Eph. 4:32).

8. "Dear children, let us not love with words or tongue but with actions and in truth" (1 John 3:18).

100
OVERCOMING OFFENSES

Heavenly Father, pour Your healing anointing into my daughter's heart. Heal and protect her from all past and future offenses.[1] Cause her to take every opportunity to avoid offenses and promote Your love which You poured into her when she was born-again.[2]

Keep her from repeating an offense, even within her heart, so she doesn't harm her relationships with her family, friends and You.[3] Thank You for Your love which prevents her from being touchy or easily angered. It prevents her from keeping an account of the wrong done to her.[4]

Help _____ to walk in Your wisdom which leads to peace.[5] May others recognize and be encouraged when she overlooks offenses.[6]

Remind my child to be kind to others, tenderhearted and forgiving, just as You have forgiven her.[7] Help her love those who wrong her, and help her prove that love with her words and actions.[8] In Jesus' name.

GOD'S WORD SAYS

1. "So don't be afraid; you are worth more than many sparrows. Whoever acknowledges me before men, I will also acknowledge him before my Father in heaven" (Matt. 10:31-32).

2. "Finally, be strong in the Lord and in his mighty power" (Eph. 6:10).

3. "Have you not put a hedge around him and his household and everything he has? You have blessed the work of his hands, so that his flocks and herds are spread throughout the land" (Job 1:10).

4. "For it is God who works in you to will and to act according to his good purpose" (Phil. 2:13).

5. "Avoid every kind of evil" (1 Thess. 5:22).

6. "I guide you in the way of wisdom and lead you along straight paths. When you walk, your steps will not be hampered; when you run, you will not stumble" (Prov. 4:11-12).

7. "Do not set foot on the path of the wicked or walk in the way of evil men. Avoid it, do not travel on it; turn from it and go on your way" (Prov. 4:14-15).

8. "Do not be afraid of those who kill the body but cannot kill the soul" (Matt. 10:28).

9. "Fear of man will prove to be a snare, but whoever trusts in the Lord is kept safe" (Prov. 29:25).

10. "Watch your life and doctrine closely. Persevere in them, because if you do, you will save both yourself and your hearers" (1 Tim. 4:16).

101

PEER PRESSURE

Heavenly Father, give _____ Your supernatural strength to overcome peer pressure. May he not be ashamed to stand up for what is right.[1] Let him be strong in You and in Your mighty power[2] even if his closest friends try to entice or manipulate him into doing wrong.

Place a hedge of protection around him,[3] protecting him from every person, place or thing that would try to hinder the work You are doing in his life.[4] Keep all evil away from him.[5] Thank You for guiding my child in the way of wisdom along straight paths,[6] not letting him walk on the path of the wicked but avoiding it and turning from it.[7]

May he not fear what his friends think about him,[8] but instead may he trust You.[9] Thank You that as he perseveres in a godly life he will be a positive influence to every one around him.[10]

God's Word Says

1.   "Brothers, choose seven men from among you who are known to be full of the Spirit and wisdom. We will turn this responsibility over to them" (Acts 6:3).

2.   "So the warden put Joseph in charge of all those held in the prison, and he was made responsible for all that was done there. The warden paid no attention to anything under Joseph's care, because the Lord was with Joseph and gave him success in whatever he did" (Gen. 39:22-23).

3.   "Those who were musicians, heads of Levite families, stayed in the rooms of the temple and were exempt from other duties because they were responsible for the work day and night" (1 Chr. 9:33).

4.   "Since they show that the requirements of the law are written on their hearts, their consciences also bearing witness, and their thoughts now accusing, now even defending them" (Rom. 2:15).

5.   "Now it is required that those who have been given a trust must prove faithful" (1 Cor. 4:2).

6.   "His master replied, 'Well done, good and faithful servant! You have been faithful with a few things; I will put you in charge of many things. Come and share your master's happiness!'" (Matt. 25:21).

102
RESPONSIBILITY

Heavenly Father, I pray that _____ will be full of Your Spirit, full of wisdom and qualified for every responsibility.[1] Thank You for keeping Your hand on my child, making her so responsible that those in authority over her don't have to badger her to complete her work. Grant her success in whatever she does![2]

In areas of our home and family I ask that You place the desire in my child to be responsible for her work both day and night.[3] Let the rules of our household be more than a law to her. Write them on her heart so that her conscience bears witness.[4]

Because she has been trusted with certain responsibilities, I pray that You will help her prove faithful in every area.[5] Thank You for causing her to be faithful even in the small things and for putting her in charge of many things.[6] In Jesus' name.

GOD'S WORD SAYS

1. "The circumcised believers who had come with Peter were astonished that the gift of the Holy Spirit had been poured out even on the Gentiles" (Acts 10:45).

2. "Don't you know that you yourselves are God's temple and that God's Spirit lives in you? If anyone destroys God's temple, God will destroy him; for God's temple is sacred, and you are that temple" (1 Cor. 3:16-17).

3. "So that you may become blameless and pure, children of God without fault in a crooked and depraved generation, in which you shine like stars in the universe" (Phil. 2:15).

4. "Above all else, guard your heart, for it is the wellspring of life" (Prov. 4:23).

5. "Everyone who has this hope in him purifies himself, just as he is pure" (1 John 3:3).

6. "No one else dared join them, even though they were highly regarded by the people. Nevertheless, more and more men and women believed in the Lord and were added to their number" (Acts 5:13-14).

7. "Don't let anyone look down on you because you are young, but set an example for the believers in speech, in life, in love, in faith and in purity" (1 Tim. 4:12).

103

Sexual Purity

Heavenly Father, thank You for the gift of the Holy Spirit that You have given my child.[1] I pray that he will walk in the full reality of the fact that his body is the temple of the Holy Spirit.[2] I praise You for the power to remain spotless in a crooked and perverse world![3] Help _____ guard his heart from anyone or anything that would try to influence him to turn loose of his sexual purity.[4]

Father, help my child keep his body pure for marriage from this day forth and to purify himself, just as You are pure.[5] Thank You that he will be an example to everyone around him, not looked down upon but respected for taking a stand for purity and holiness.[6] Let him be an example in speech, life, love, faith and purity to all of his peers.[7] In Jesus' name.

God's Word Says

1. "But the fruit of the Spirit is love, joy, peace, patience, kindness, goodness, faithfulness, gentleness and self-control. Against such things there is no law" (Gal. 5:22-23).

2. "Also in Judah the hand of God was on the people to give them unity of mind to carry out what the king and his officials had ordered, following the word of the Lord" (2 Chr. 30:12).

3. "How good and pleasant it is when brothers live together in unity! It is like precious oil poured on the head, running down on the beard, running down on Aaron's beard, down upon the collar of his robes. It is as if the dew of Hermon were falling on Mount Zion. For there the Lord bestows his blessing, even life forevermore" (Ps. 133:1-3).

4. "I in them and you in me. May they be brought to complete unity to let the world know that you sent me and have loved them even as you have loved me" (John 17:23).

5. "May the God who gives endurance and encouragement give you a spirit of unity among yourselves as you follow Christ Jesus, so that with one heart and mouth you may glorify the God and Father of our Lord Jesus Christ" (Rom. 15:5-6).

6. "Be completely humble and gentle; be patient, bearing with one another in love. Make every effort to keep the unity of the Spirit through the bond of peace" (Eph. 4:2-3).

7. "Until we all reach unity in the faith and in the knowledge of the Son of God and become mature, attaining to the whole measure of the fullness of Christ" (Eph. 4:13).

104
SIBLING RELATIONSHIPS

Father, I pray that our family will show the fruit of the Spirit in our lives toward one another, allowing Your love, joy, peace, patience, kindness, goodness, faithfulness, gentleness and self-control to be manifested in our lives.[1]

Thank You that Your Spirit rests upon my children, giving them unity to carry out the guidelines of our home as they follow Your Word.[2] Your Word says it is good and pleasant when brothers live together in unity! I release Your unity to completely saturate my children with blessings and life.[3] Thank You for the example of unity You gave in Jesus.[4]

I ask that Your endurance and encouragement will rest on my home and family. In Jesus' name I proclaim that my family has one heartbeat to glorify You![5] I pray that my children will live in godly humility with one another, being patient and loving with each other. Help them to make every effort to strengthen the bond of peace in our family,[6] which leads to maturity and fullness in You.[7] In Jesus' name.

GOD'S WORD SAYS

1. "Therefore confess your sins to each other and pray for each other so that you may be healed. The prayer of a righteous man is powerful and effective" (James 5:16).

2. "Plans fail for lack of counsel, but with many advisers they succeed" (Prov. 15:22).

3. "Not lording it over those entrusted to you, but being examples to the flock. And when the Chief Shepherd appears, you will receive the crown of glory that will never fade away. Young men, in the same way be submissive to those who are older. All of you, clothe yourselves with humility toward one another, because, 'God opposes the proud but gives grace to the humble'" (1 Pet. 5:3-5).

   "He taught me and said, 'Lay hold of my words with all your heart; keep my commands and you will live'" (Prov. 4:4).

4. "Do not be anxious about anything, but in everything, by prayer and petition, with thanksgiving, present your requests to God. And the peace of God, which transcends all understanding, will guard your hearts and your minds in Christ Jesus" (Phil. 4:6-7).

105
SUPPORT

Heavenly Father, I pray that I will be supportive as a parent to _____. Help me be sensitive to the trials and temptations he may be facing, and with that sensitivity I will accept the responsibility to pray effectively for him.[1]

Thank You for surrounding him with friends, relatives and people in leadership that will provide godly support and encouragement.[2] I praise You, Lord, that the people You surround him with will help to mold him into Your image and give Spirit-led instructions to him.[3] Thank You, Lord, that the decisions and choices he makes will be tempered by Your Word, prayer and wisdom.[4] In Jesus' name.

GOD'S WORD SAYS

1. "I will give you the keys of the kingdom of heaven; whatever you bind on earth will be bound in heaven, and whatever you loose on earth will be loosed in heaven" (Matt. 16:19).

2. "Every good and perfect gift is from above, coming down from the Father of the heavenly lights, who does not change like shifting shadows" (James 1:17).

3. "Then no harm will befall you, no disaster will come near your tent. For he will command his angels concerning you to guard you in all your ways" (Ps. 91:10-11).

4. "He who walks with the wise grows wise, but a companion of fools suffers harm" (Prov. 13:20).

5. "Above all else, guard your heart, for it is the wellspring of life" (Prov. 4:23).

6. "Do not swerve to the right or the left; keep your foot from evil" (Prov. 4:27).

7. "For the Lord watches over the way of the righteous, but the way of the wicked will perish" (Ps. 1:6).

106

UNGODLY RELATIONSHIPS

I bind every ungodly influence[1] that would prevent my child from receiving the good and perfect gifts God would have for her.[2] Father, I pray that You will protect her from every influence and person that would try to bring harm to her.[3]

May _____ walk with those who are wise so that she will grow in wisdom. Cause her to avoid the companionship of fools and the harm they bring.[4]

Guard my child's heart today against the agony of ungodly relationships, for her heart is the wellspring of life.[5] Keep her from swerving to the right or left of Your perfect plan.[6] Thank You that my child will not perish in the way of the ungodly but can rest in the confidence that You will show her the way she is to go.[7] In Jesus' name.

GOD'S WORD SAYS

1. "He whose walk is blameless and who does what is righteous, who speaks the truth from his heart and has no slander on his tongue, who does his neighbor no wrong and casts no slur on his fellow-man" (Ps. 15:2-3).

2. "When pride comes, then comes disgrace, but with humility comes wisdom" (Prov. 11:2).

3. "I know, my God, that you test the heart and are pleased with integrity. All these things have I given willingly and with honest intent. And now I have seen with joy how willingly your people who are here have given to you" (1 Chr. 29:17).

4. "Therefore, since we are surrounded by such a great cloud of witnesses, let us throw off everything that hinders and the sin that so easily entangles, and let us run with perseverance the race marked out for us" (Heb. 12:1).

5. "Your word is a lamp to my feet and a light for my path" (Ps. 119:105).

6. "Therefore, get rid of all moral filth and the evil that is so prevalent and humbly accept the word planted in you, which can save you" (James 1:21).

107
VALUES

Thank You, heavenly Father, for guiding the values of my child. I proclaim that my child has right standing with You and therefore prizes honesty and is careful always to speak highly of others.[1] Thank You for making my child truly humble and saturating him with Your wisdom.[2] Make _____ a person of his word, for I know that You test the heart and are pleased with integrity.[3]

Help him to throw off any hindrances that would be an entanglement to trap him. Put within him the desire to run a race of faith with perseverance.[4] I pray that You will help him persevere through all circumstances so that his character may become solid and unshakable. Your Word is a light for his feet and a lamp that illuminates the path he takes.[5] Thank You that he humbly accepts the Word planted within to shape his values.[6]

Section IV

SCHOOL NEEDS

GOD'S WORD SAYS

1. "Esteem her, and she will exalt you; embrace her, and she will honor you" (Prov. 4:8).

2. "'For who has known the mind of the Lord that he may instruct him?' But we have the mind of Christ" (1 Cor. 2:16).

3. "And I have filled him with the Spirit of God, with skill, ability and knowledge in all kinds of crafts" (Ex. 31:3).

4. "The sluggard craves and gets nothing, but the desires of the diligent are fully satisfied" (Prov. 13:4).

5. "Whatever you do, work at it with all your heart, as working for the Lord, not for men" (Col. 3:23).

6. "May the favor of the Lord our God rest upon us; establish the work of our hands for us — yes, establish the work of our hands" (Ps. 90:17).

7. "A man can do nothing better than to eat and drink and find satisfaction in his work. This too, I see, is from the hand of God" (Eccl. 2:24).

108
ACADEMIC ACHIEVEMENTS

Heavenly Father, I ask You to put a consuming desire for wisdom in _____. As he sets his hand to attain wisdom, thank You for promoting and prospering him[1] because he has the mind of Christ.[2] Thank You that his skills, abilities and knowledge come from You.[3] Let my child's desire for academic achievement be fully satisfied because of his diligence.[4]

I pray that he will practice obedience — really trying — not only when others' eyes are on him but at all times with sincerity of heart and a genuine reverence for Your ways. I pray he will work with all of his heart in his studies because he is really working for You and not for men.[5] You, and You alone, establish the work of his hands, allowing Your favor to rest upon him in all he does.[6] Let him see the fruit of his studies, and encourage him through the enjoyment of his labor.[7] In Jesus' name.

God's Word Says

1. "May integrity and uprightness protect me, because my hope is in you" (Ps. 25:21).

2 "No temptation has seized you except what is common to man. And God is faithful; he will not let you be tempted beyond what you can bear. But when you are tempted, he will also provide a way out so that you can stand up under it" (1 Cor. 10:13).

3. "The man of integrity walks securely, but he who takes crooked paths will be found out" (Prov. 10:9).

4. "The integrity of the upright guides them, but the unfaithful are destroyed by their duplicity" (Prov. 11:3).

5. "Then you will know the truth, and the truth will set you free" (John 8:32).

6. "And my honesty will testify for me in the future, whenever you check on the wages you have paid me" (Gen. 30:33).

7. "I know, my God, that you test the heart and are pleased with integrity. All these things have I given willingly and with honest intent. And now I have seen with joy how willingly your people who are here have given to you" (1 Chr. 29:17).

109
CHEATING

Heavenly Father, cause integrity and uprightness to protect my child because her hope is in You.[1] I pray against the temptation for her to cheat in her studies, knowing that You always provide a way to escape that temptation.[2] Help her to walk securely, avoiding crooked paths, demonstrating Your integrity within.[3]

Lord, let Your honesty be a guide to _____. Keep her from duplicity and compromise so that her character is not tainted or destroyed.[4] Thank You that she will practice the truth; that the truth always sets her free![5] Let her honesty be a testimony of her good character,[6] bringing glory to Your name. I know You test the hearts of men, and so You will be pleased with my child's integrity as she serves You.[7] In Jesus' name.

God's Word Says

1. "Trust in the Lord with all your heart and lean not on your own understanding; in all your ways acknowledge him, and he will make your paths straight" (Prov. 3:5-6).

2. "I tell you the truth, whatever you bind on earth will be bound in heaven, and whatever you loose on earth will be loosed in heaven" (Matt. 18:18).

3. "You are my lamp, O Lord; the Lord turns my darkness into light" (2 Sam. 22:29).

4. "I will instruct you and teach you in the way you should go; I will counsel you and watch over you" (Ps. 32:8).

5. "If the Lord delights in a man's way, he makes his steps firm" (Ps. 37:23).

6. "The Lord himself goes before you and will be with you; he will never leave you nor forsake you. Do not be afraid; do not be discouraged" (Deut. 31:8).

7. "For the Lord gives wisdom, and from his mouth come knowledge and understanding" (Prov. 2:6).

8. "Let the peace of Christ rule in your hearts, since as members of one body you were called to peace. And be thankful" (Col. 3:15).

110

Choosing a College

Heavenly Father, I pray that my child will not depend on his own understanding with the very important decision of choosing a college. Rather, may he trust in You and acknowledge Your control so the path he takes is straight and clear.[1] I bind indecision and confusion.[2] Bring illumination to his decisions and make his darkness bright.[3]

Thank You for instructing and guiding _____ along the best pathway for his life. I praise You for advising him and watching over his progress.[4] You have ordered every one of his steps.[5] He will not fear, for You go before him in all situations. Make it more than apparent that You will neither fail nor forsake him.[6]

As he meditates on Your every word, thank You that he will find the treasures of knowledge and understanding about which steps to take,[7] for Your peace rules his heart in this matter.[8] You are revealing to him which college to attend. In Jesus' name.

God's Word Says

1. "Delight yourself in the Lord and he will give you the desires of your heart" (Ps. 37:4).

2. "'For I know the plans I have for you,' declares the Lord, 'plans to prosper you and not to harm you, plans to give you hope and a future'" (Jer. 29:11).

3. "Therefore do not be foolish, but understand what the Lord's will is" (Eph. 5:17).

4. "Whether you turn to the right or to the left, your ears will hear a voice behind you, saying, 'This is the way; walk in it'" (Is. 30:21).

5. "Do not be like them, for your Father knows what you need before you ask him" (Matt. 6:8).

   "Then he said: 'The God of our fathers has chosen you to know his will and to see the Righteous One and to hear words from his mouth'" (Acts 22:14).

6. "'For who has known the mind of the Lord that he may instruct him?' But we have the mind of Christ" (1 Cor. 2:16).

7. "Because those who are led by the Spirit of God are sons of God" (Rom. 8:14).

111
CHOOSING A MAJOR

Heavenly Father, thank You for placing Your desires for my child's life directly into her heart and for making them come to pass.[1] Reveal the plans You have for my child, giving her hope and a future.[2] When deciding on a college major, my child will not be foolish but will understand what Your will is for her life.[3]

I praise You that even if my child should choose the wrong major at first, You will speak to her, saying, "No, this is the way — walk here."[4] Help _____ to remember that You know exactly what she needs even before she asks You.[5] You have chosen to give my child the very mind of Christ,[6] and she is led by Your Spirit in this matter![7] In Jesus' name.

God's Word Says

1. "It is because of him that you are in Christ Jesus, who has become for us wisdom from God — that is, our righteousness, holiness and redemption" (1 Cor. 1:30).

2. "Delight yourself in the Lord and he will give you the desires of your heart" (Ps. 37:4).

3. "Blessed is the man who does not walk in the counsel of the wicked or stand in the way of sinners or sit in the seat of mockers. But his delight is in the law of the Lord, and on his law he meditates day and night. He is like a tree planted by streams of water, which yields its fruit in season and whose leaf does not wither. Whatever he does prospers" (Ps. 1:1-3).

4. "He who walks with the wise grows wise, but a companion of fools suffers harm" (Prov. 13:20).

5. "Flee the evil desires of youth, and pursue righteousness, faith, love and peace, along with those who call on the Lord out of a pure heart" (2 Tim. 2:22).

6. "Thus you will walk in the ways of good men and keep to the paths of the righteous" (Prov. 2:20).

7. "Two are better than one, because they have a good return for their work" (Eccl. 4:9).

112
CHOOSING FRIENDS

Father, thank You for giving _____ wisdom in choosing his friends.[1] I pray that You will bring godly people and influences into his life. Put in his heart a desire for quality friendships.[2] May he not seek wisdom from bad influences, hang out with godless people or join in with people who are cruel.[3] Instead of choosing companions who are foolish, I pray that he will choose to be around those who practice wisdom.[4]

I pray he will use the characteristics of righteousness, faith, love and peace to discern the right people to associate with. May he seek those who call on You with a pure heart.[5] Keep him in the paths of good influences.[6] Thank You for the special friends You are bringing across his path to help and encourage him.[7] In Jesus' name.

God's Word Says

1. "For it is by grace you have been saved, through faith — and this not from yourselves, it is the gift of God" (Eph. 2:8).

2. "Don't let anyone look down on you because you are young, but set an example for the believers in speech, in life, in love, in faith and in purity" (1 Tim. 4:12).

3. "You are the light of the world. A city on a hill cannot be hidden. Neither do people light a lamp and put it under a bowl. Instead they put it on its stand, and it gives light to everyone in the house" (Matt. 5:14-15).

4. "Fear of man will prove to be a snare, but whoever trusts in the Lord is kept safe" (Prov. 29:25).

5. "I am not ashamed of the gospel, because it is the power of God for the salvation of everyone who believes: first for the Jew, then for the Gentile" (Rom. 1:16).

6. "Do not forsake your friend and the friend of your father, and do not go to your brother's house when disaster strikes you — better a neighbor nearby than a brother far away" (Prov. 27:10).

7. "Be kind and compassionate to one another, forgiving each other, just as in Christ God forgave you" (Eph. 4:32).

8. "By this all men will know that you are my disciples, if you love one another" (John 13:35).

9. "Let love and faithfulness never leave you; bind them around your neck, write them on the tablet of your heart. Then you will win favor and a good name in the sight of God and man" (Prov. 3:3-4).

113
CHRISTIAN WITNESS

Heavenly Father, thank You that _____ has trusted Jesus with her life and has been saved by Your kindness and grace. Salvation is Your gift to her,[1] and I ask You to help her give this gift away to others. Help her to be an example to others in everything she does: in her words, her conduct and her attitude.[2]

You have called her to be the light to the world, as a city on a hill that can't be hidden. Give her the boldness to let her lamp shine before everyone so they will glorify You because of her good works.[3] Keep her free from the fear of men.[4] She will not be ashamed of the gospel because it is the power of God unto salvation.[5]

Cause her to be a faithful friend,[6] striving to be kind to others.[7] Allow them to see her love for people so they will know she is Your disciple.[8] Show _____ how to walk in love at all times and be a true friend to people so that she may win a good name with You as well as with others.[9]

GOD'S WORD SAYS

1. "Equip you with everything good for doing his will, and may he work in us what is pleasing to him, through Jesus Christ, to whom be glory for ever and ever. Amen" (Heb. 13:21).

2. "A simple man believes anything, but a prudent man gives thought to his steps" (Prov. 14:15).

3. "Therefore put on the full armor of God, so that when the day of evil comes, you may be able to stand your ground, and after you have done everything, to stand" (Eph. 6:13).

4. "Epaphras, who is one of you and a servant of Christ Jesus, sends greetings. He is always wrestling in prayer for you, that you may stand firm in all the will of God, mature and fully assured" (Col. 4:12).

5. "I will instruct you and teach you in the way you should go; I will counsel you and watch over you" (Ps. 32:8).

6. "Suppose one of you wants to build a tower. Will he not first sit down and estimate the cost to see if he has enough money to complete it? For if he lays the foundation and is not able to finish it, everyone who sees it will ridicule him" (Luke 14:28-29).

7. "Commit to the Lord whatever you do, and your plans will succeed" (Prov. 16:3).

114

COLLEGE PREPAREDNESS

Father, I pray that my child will be equipped with everything good for doing Your will. Work within him so that he may be pleasing to You as he prepares for college.[1] Thank You for causing him to give careful thought and consideration to the steps that are set before him.[2]

I pray that he will put on the full armor of God so that he can stand his ground against the devil as he goes on to college.[3] Keep _____ standing firm in Your will, mature and fully assured of the plan You have for him.[4]

Thank You for instructing and advising my child, watching his progress carefully.[5] Help him to estimate the cost of his education carefully to be sure he is able to finish it.[6] Prepare him for what will be required of him when he arrives at college. I ask You to meet him where he is right now, helping him to commit his work to You so that it will succeed.[7] In Jesus' name.

GOD'S WORD SAYS

1. "Remember your Creator in the days of your youth, before the days of trouble come and the years approach when you will say, 'I find no pleasure in them'" (Eccl. 12:1).

2. "Shout for joy to the Lord, all the earth...Know that the Lord is God. It is he who made us, and we are his; we are his people, the sheep of his pasture" (Ps. 100:1,3).

3. "So God created man in his own image, in the image of God he created him; male and female he created them" (Gen. 1:27).

4. "I pray also that the eyes of your heart may be enlightened in order that you may know the hope to which he has called you, the riches of his glorious inheritance in the saints" (Eph. 1:18).

5. "For since the creation of the world God's invisible qualities — his eternal power and divine nature — have been clearly seen, being understood from what has been made, so that men are without excuse" (Rom. 1:20).

6. "Stand firm then, with the belt of truth buckled around your waist, with the breastplate of righteousness in place" (Eph. 6:14).

7. "Avoid godless chatter, because those who indulge in it will become more and more ungodly" (2 Tim. 2:16).

8. "After they prayed, the place where they were meeting was shaken. And they were all filled with the Holy Spirit and spoke the word of God boldly" (Acts 4:31).

115
EVOLUTION/CREATION ISSUES

Heavenly Father, thank You for revealing to my child the truth about Your creation. Thank You that she knows You as Creator.[1] Let Your Holy Spirit witness to her heart that life is not an accident — You made us.[2] You created my child in Your image.[3] Keep the eyes of her understanding open toward You[4] so that she can clearly see and understand Your eternal power and divine nature at work in her life.[5]

I pray that _____ will be armed with the belt of Your truth[6] so that she can recognize the godless philosophies of man.[7] Thank You for filling my child with Your Holy Spirit so she can speak the Word of God boldly about Your creation.[8]

GOD'S WORD SAYS

1. "Do not conform any longer to the pattern of this world, but be transformed by the renewing of your mind. Then you will be able to test and approve what God's will is — his good, pleasing and perfect will" (Rom. 12:2).

2. "Whoever obeys his command will come to no harm, and the wise heart will know the proper time and procedure" (Eccl. 8:5).

3. "Better one handful with tranquillity than two handfuls with toil and chasing after the wind" (Eccl. 4:6).

4. "But the wisdom that comes from heaven is first of all pure; then peace-loving, considerate, submissive, full of mercy and good fruit, impartial and sincere" (James 3:17).

5. "Come near to God and he will come near to you. Wash your hands, you sinners, and purify your hearts, you double-minded" (James 4:8).

6. "But seek first his kingdom and his righteousness, and all these things will be given to you as well" (Matt. 6:33).

116

EXTRA-CURRICULAR ACTIVITIES

Heavenly Father, I praise You that my child's mind is being renewed by Your Word, making him fully capable to perform Your good and perfect will in every area of his life, including his extra-curricular activities.[1]

May he be discerning to use his time properly. Help him understand how to fit activities into his schedule realistically.[2] Keep him from taking on so much that peace eludes him. Don't let him get so busy with extra things that he becomes discouraged and feels that he's chasing after the wind.[3]

As _____ exercises wisdom and discipline in this area, let him experience Your peace and the good fruit You promise.[4] I pray that keeping his priorities right with You will be the most important factor in his decisions about extra-curricular events.

Draw close to him as he draws close to You.[5] May he seek Your kingdom and Your righteousness first, and You will add everything else unto him.[6] In Jesus' name.

GOD'S WORD SAYS

1. "For the Lord God is a sun and shield; the Lord bestows favor and honor; no good thing does he withhold from those whose walk is blameless" (Ps. 84:11).

2. "Moses said to the Lord, 'You have been telling me, Lead these people, but you have not let me know whom you will send with me. You have said, I know you by name and you have found favor with me'" (Ex. 33:12).

3. "Let love and faithfulness never leave you; bind them around your neck, write them on the tablet of your heart. Then you will win favor and a good name in the sight of God and man" (Prov. 3:3-4).

4. "He who rebukes a man will in the end gain more favor than he who has a flattering tongue" (Prov. 28:23).

5. "After Job had prayed for his friends, the Lord made him prosperous again and gave him twice as much as he had before" (Job 42:10).

117

FAVOR AMONG PEERS

Heavenly Father, You are as bright as the sun in my child's life, and You protect her like a shield. You bestow favor and honor on her with her peers and do not withhold any good thing from her.[1] You know her by name, and she has Your endless favor.[2]

Show _____ how to walk in love at all times and how to be a true friend to everyone so that she may win a good name with You as well as with others.[3] Keep her from unnecessary flattery, sticking to what she believes in at all cost.[4]

Teach her to follow godly examples, praying for her friends' needs instead of just her own. May she recognize the value You place upon friendship as You prosper her for her faithfulness to her friends.[5] In Jesus' name.

God's Word Says

1. "And David shepherded them with integrity of heart; with skillful hands he led them" (Ps. 78:72).

2. "I will look on you with favor and make you fruitful and increase your numbers, and I will keep my covenant with you" (Lev. 26:9).

3. "Whatever you do, work at it with all your heart, as working for the Lord, not for men" (Col. 3:23).

4. "I also told them about the gracious hand of my God upon me and what the king had said to me. They replied, 'Let us start rebuilding.' So they began this good work" (Neh. 2:18).

5. "Let love and faithfulness never leave you; bind them around your neck, write them on the tablet of your heart. Then you will win favor and a good name in the sight of God and man" (Prov. 3:3-4).

6. "Obey them not only to win their favor when their eye is on you, but like slaves of Christ, doing the will of God from your heart" (Eph. 6:6).

118

FAVOR IN SPORTS

Heavenly Father, thank You that _____ has Your divine favor on his life, including favor with his coaches and teammates. Make him a leader like David who led others with integrity of heart and skillful hands.[1] Because of Your favor, my child will be made fruitful in this area.[2]

I pray that my child will work at sports with all of his heart, working for You and not just for the praises of men.[3] Like the builders of the wall of Jerusalem, may he and his teammates sense Your hand upon them in every sports event.[4] Help him to walk in love at all times. Teach him faithfulness to his teammates, coaches and sport so that he can win a good name in Your eyes and in theirs.[5] I pray that he will work hard not only to win the favor of his coaches and teammates but because he wants to do Your will.[6] In Jesus' name.

GOD'S WORD SAYS

1. "And he said to man, 'The fear of the Lord — that is wisdom, and to shun evil is understanding" (Job 28:28).

2. "Listen to me; be silent, and I will teach you wisdom" (Job 33:33).

3. "Study to shew thyself approved unto God, a workman that needeth not to be ashamed, rightly dividing the word of truth" (2 Tim. 2:15, KJV).

4. "But the Comforter, which is the Holy Ghost, whom the Father will send in my name, he shall teach you all things, and bring all things to your remembrance, whatsoever I have said unto you" (John 14:26).

5. "God is our refuge and strength, an ever-present help in trouble" (Ps. 46:1).

6. "For God did not give us a spirit of timidity, but a spirit of power, of love and of self-discipline" (2 Tim. 1:7).

7. "So do not fear, for I am with you; do not be dismayed, for I am your God. I will strengthen you and help you; I will uphold you with my righteous right hand" (Is. 41:10).

119
Help for Tests and Exams

Heavenly Father, thank You that the fear of the Lord brings wisdom, and shunning evil brings understanding.[1] Give my child a calm spirit so that she may be silent before You and You can teach her wisdom.[2] Thank You for teaching her to study diligently so she does not need to be ashamed of her work, comprehending the truth on her tests and exams.[3] Give her supernatural recall for the things she studied.[4]

You are a very present help in _____'s time of need.[5] You have not given her a spirit of fear but of power, love and a sound mind.[6] Thank You for being with her as she takes her exams. She doesn't need to be dismayed, for You strengthen and help her. You uphold her with Your victorious right hand.[7] In Jesus' name.

GOD'S WORD SAYS

1. "May the favor of the Lord our God rest upon us; establish the work of our hands for us — yes, establish the work of our hands" (Ps. 90:17).

2. "Whatever you do, work at it with all your heart, as working for the Lord, not for men" (Col. 3:23).

3. "Commit to the Lord whatever you do, and your plans will succeed" (Prov. 16:3).

4. "I guide you in the way of wisdom and lead you along straight paths" (Prov. 4:11).

5. "Wise men store up knowledge, but the mouth of a fool invites ruin" (Prov. 10:14).

6. "The heart of the discerning acquires knowledge; the ears of the wise seek it out" (Prov. 18:15).

7. "I can do everything through him who gives me strength" (Phil. 4:13).

120
HOMEWORK

Heavenly Father, I pray that the work of _____'s hands would be established.[1] I ask that You would cause him to obey his teacher's rules and complete every assignment. He doesn't do this just to win their favor, but he works with all his heart, truly working for You, not just for men.[2] When he commits his work to You his plans are guaranteed to succeed.[3] Thank You for leading him in the way of wisdom and making his paths upright.[4]

Help my child understand the importance of storing up knowledge by completing his homework.[5] Give him discernment and good listening skills in his classes so that he will be prepared to do his work.[6]

I praise You for giving him Your supernatural strength to complete each task set before him. He can do all things through Christ who is his strength![7] In Jesus' name.

God's Word Says

1. "Avoid godless chatter, because those who indulge in it will become more and more ungodly" (2 Tim. 2:16).

2. "For giving prudence to the simple, knowledge and discretion to the young — let the wise listen and add to their learning, and let the discerning get guidance" (Prov. 1:4-5).

3. "The wages of the righteous bring them life, but the income of the wicked brings them punishment" (Prov. 10:16).

4. "Whoever loves discipline loves knowledge, but he who hates correction is stupid" (Prov. 12:1).

5. "I pray also that the eyes of your heart may be enlightened in order that you may know the hope to which he has called you, the riches of his glorious inheritance in the saints" (Eph. 1:18).

6. "No discipline seems pleasant at the time, but painful. Later on, however, it produces a harvest of righteousness and peace for those who have been trained by it" (Heb. 12:11).

121

MAINTAINING GOOD GRADES

Heavenly Father, I pray that You will help my child maintain her grades. May she refuse to give her time to disruptions and inattentiveness.[1] Keep her mind focused so as to be prudent, gaining knowledge and discretion. Make her wise to gain understanding from her teachers and subject matter.[2]

Father, cause _____ to be a good example of discipline, good grades and comprehension of the way to life to her peers.[3] Make her a lover of discipline and a lover of knowledge.[4] Even though the discipline to maintain good grades seems painful at times, I pray that You will open the eyes of her understanding[5] to see that godly discipline produces a harvest of righteousness and peace for those who have been trained by it.[6] In Jesus' name.

GOD'S WORD SAYS

1. "I pray also that the eyes of your heart may be enlightened in order that you may know the hope to which he has called you, the riches of his glorious inheritance in the saints" (Eph. 1:18).

2. "He has showed you, O man, what is good. And what does the Lord require of you? To act justly and to love mercy and to walk humbly with your God" (Mic. 6:8).

3. "If you really change your ways and your actions and deal with each other justly, if you do not oppress the alien, the fatherless or the widow and do not shed innocent blood in this place, and if you do not follow other gods to your own harm" (Jer. 7:5-6).

4. "And we urge you, brothers, warn those who are idle, encourage the timid, help the weak, be patient with everyone" (1 Thess. 5:14).

5. "Do not pervert justice; do not show partiality to the poor or favoritism to the great, but judge your neighbor fairly" (Lev. 19:15).

6. "Whenever the Lord raised up a judge for them, he was with the judge and saved them out of the hands of their enemies as long as the judge lived; for the Lord had compassion on them as they groaned under those who oppressed and afflicted them" (Judg. 2:18).

7. "Yet the Lord longs to be gracious to you; he rises to show you compassion. For the Lord is a God of justice. Blessed are all who wait for him!" (Is. 30:18).

8. "Who comforts us in all our troubles, so that we can comfort those in any trouble with the comfort we ourselves have received from God" (2 Cor. 1:4).

9. "Therefore, as God's chosen people, holy and dearly loved, clothe yourselves with compassion, kindness, humility, gentleness and patience" (Col. 3:12).

122
OVERCOMING PREJUDICE

Heavenly Father, I ask that You open the eyes of my son's understanding[1] causing him to grasp that as a child of God You expect him to act justly, to love mercy and to walk humbly with You.[2] I rebuke prejudice and declare it has no part in his life. Let him deal fairly and equally with all men, not oppressing those who might be different than him.[3] Make _____ a friend to others so that he can encourage the timid, help the weak and exercise patience.[4] May he never show partiality or favoritism but be fair to all.[5]

I pray, Father, that he will be moved with compassion for those who are oppressed by others.[6] May he be gracious, merciful and full of justice.[7] Show him how to comfort those troubled by prejudice with the very comfort he has received from You.[8] Clothe him with compassion, kindness, humility, gentleness and patience.[9] In Jesus' name.

God's Word Says

1. "For the Lord God is a sun and shield; the Lord bestows favor and honor; no good thing does he withhold from those whose walk is blameless" (Ps. 84:11).

2. "Dear children, let us not love with words or tongue but with actions and in truth" (1 John 3:18).

3. "Blessed are the peacemakers, for they will be called sons of God. Blessed are those who are persecuted because of righteousness, for theirs is the kingdom of heaven" (Matt. 5:9-10).

4. "Although he was a son, he learned obedience from what he suffered" (Heb. 5:8).

5. "Each of you must respect his mother and father, and you must observe my Sabbaths. I am the Lord your God" (Lev. 19:3).

6. "Blessed is the man who does not walk in the counsel of the wicked or stand in the way of sinners or sit in the seat of mockers" (Ps. 1:1).

123
TEACHER RELATIONSHIPS

Thank You, Father, that my child receives every honor and good thing imaginable because of the favor You pour out upon his relationships with his teachers.[1] I pray that my child would not use empty words to obtain favor from his teachers but that he will really love and respect them with the love of Christ and show it daily by his actions.[2] I pray that as a child of God _____ will strive for peace with every teacher, even when he may feel mistreated.[3]

I ask that he will follow Christ's example of obedience, despite the possibility of adverse circumstances.[4] Give my child the courage to practice respect.[5] Keep him from following the crowd and sitting around with people who mock and make fun of those in authority.[6] In Jesus' name.

Section V

LIFE SKILLS

GOD'S WORD SAYS

1. "Every good and perfect gift is from above, coming down from the Father of the heavenly lights, who does not change like shifting shadows" (James 1:17).

2. "And my God will meet all your needs according to his glorious riches in Christ Jesus" (Phil. 4:19).

3. "You will be made rich in every way so that you can be generous on every occasion, and through us your generosity will result in thanksgiving to God" (2 Cor. 9:11).

4. "Only the Lord give thee wisdom and understanding, and give thee charge concerning Israel, that thou mayest keep the law of the Lord thy God" (1 Chr. 22:12, KJV).

5. "For the Lord gives wisdom, and from his mouth come knowledge and understanding" (Prov. 2:6).

6. "The proverbs of Solomon son of David, king of Israel: for attaining wisdom and discipline; for understanding words of insight; for acquiring a disciplined and prudent life, doing what is right and just and fair; for giving prudence to the simple, knowledge and discretion to the young — let the wise listen and add to their learning, and let the discerning get guidance" (Prov. 1:1-5).

7. "The Lord answered, 'Who then is the faithful and wise manager, whom the master puts in charge of his servants to give them their food allowance at the proper time?'" (Luke 12:42).

8. "Study to shew thyself approved unto God, a workman that needeth not to be ashamed, rightly dividing the word of truth" (2 Tim. 2:15, KJV).

124

BUDGETING FINANCES

Heavenly Father, You are *Jehovah Jireh,* the Lord my provider. Thank You, Lord, that You provide every good and perfect gift to my child.[1] Thank You, Jesus, for supplying all of his needs according to Your riches in glory[2] and for making him prosperous in every way so he can have a surplus with which to be generous on every occasion.[3]

Jesus, I ask for Your wisdom and understanding about finances to flow through _____.[4] Give him ideas and witty inventions that will produce increase to bless him and others around him.[5] I'm asking You today to give _____ wisdom in the area of discipline and budgeting.[6] Make him a good steward of his money.[7] I pray that he will learn how to handle his finances efficiently. Father, place in him the desire to study stewardship.[8] Thank You that he will not be foolish concerning money. Bless him with wisdom right now. In Jesus' name!

GOD'S WORD SAYS

1. "If the Lord delights in a man's way, he makes his steps firm" (Ps. 37:23).

2. "'For I know the plans I have for you,' declares the Lord, 'plans to prosper you and not to harm you, plans to give you hope and a future'" (Jer. 29:11).

3. "Do not conform any longer to the pattern of this world, but be transformed by the renewing of your mind. Then you will be able to test and approve what God's will is — his good, pleasing and perfect will" (Rom. 12:2).

4. "For God is not the author of confusion, but of peace, as in all churches of the saints" (1 Cor. 14:33, KJV).

5. "For if you remain silent at this time, relief and deliverance for the Jews will arise from another place, but you and your father's family will perish. And who knows but that you have come to royal position for such a time as this?" (Esth. 4:14).

6. "For surely, O Lord, you bless the righteous; you surround them with your favor as with a shield" (Ps. 5:12).

7. "Because a great door for effective work has opened to me, and there are many who oppose me" (1 Cor. 16:9).

125
CAREER CHOICES

Heavenly Father, thank You for giving my daughter direction regarding the career choice to pursue, for You are ordering her steps and placing Your desires in her heart.[1] Thank You for the plan You have for _____'s life to prosper her, a plan of hope and a good future.[2] Thank You for opening the eyes of her understanding and showing her what Your good and perfect will is for her life.[3] Give her revelation and understanding about what to do! Give her a clear understanding and a singleness of mind, for You are not the author of confusion.[4] Let her mind be alert and her heart receptive in Your mighty name!

I ask that this will be a special time in my child's life as she prepares herself for her ultimate destiny. Thank You, Father, for preparing my child for such a time as this.[5] And Lord, as she steps into her career, thank You for surrounding her with favor like a shield.[6] Thank You for opening up effective doors of opportunity for her today.[7]

God's Word Says

1. "Because those who are led by the Spirit of God are sons of God" (Rom. 8:14).

2. "I love those who love me, and those who seek me find me" (Prov. 8:17).

3. "You will seek me and find me when you seek me with all your heart" (Jer. 29:13).

4. "Since you are my rock and my fortress, for the sake of your name lead and guide me" (Ps. 31:3).

5. "Whoever obeys his command will come to no harm, and the wise heart will know the proper time and procedure. For there is a proper time and procedure for every matter, though a man's misery weighs heavily upon him" (Eccl. 8:5-6).

6. "When he has brought out all his own, he goes on ahead of them, and his sheep follow him because they know his voice" (John 10:4).

7. "Therefore, I urge you, brothers, in view of God's mercy, to offer your bodies as living sacrifices, holy and pleasing to God — this is your spiritual act of worship. Do not conform any longer to the pattern of this world, but be transformed by the renewing of your mind. Then you will be able to test and approve what God's will is — his good, pleasing and perfect will" (Rom. 12:1-2).

126
DIRECTION

Dear heavenly Father, I just want to praise You today for the privileges of being a child of God. Thank You that one of those privileges is being led by Your Spirit.[1] Urge my child to seek direction from You;[2] for as he seeks You, he will find You.[3] As _____ seeks You, Lord, he will know exactly what plans to pursue. Help him to recognize that You are his rock and fortress, and You will lead and guide his life.[4]

Father, thank You for Your timing and Your procedure for everything.[5] I ask that Your Spirit will be so real to him that he will be sensitive to Your voice[6] and will pursue the direction You have for him. Help him to conform to Your image and to renew his mind so he will know what Your good and perfect will is for every step of his life.[7] Thank You for causing my son to walk in Your will with confidence and boldness. In Jesus' name!

GOD'S WORD SAYS

1. "As iron sharpens iron, so one man sharpens another" (Prov. 27:17).

2. "Submit yourselves for the Lord's sake to every authority instituted among men: whether to the king, as the supreme authority...Slaves, submit yourselves to your masters with all respect, not only to those who are good and considerate, but also to those who are harsh" (1 Pet. 2:13,18).

3. "Don't let anyone look down on you because you are young, but set an example for the believers in speech, in life, in love, in faith and in purity" (1 Tim. 4:12).

4. "In the same way, let your light shine before men, that they may see your good deeds and praise your Father in heaven" (Matt. 5:16).

5. "For surely, O Lord, you bless the righteous; you surround them with your favor as with a shield" (Ps. 5:12).

127
EMPLOYER/EMPLOYEE RELATIONSHIPS

Heavenly Father, I lift up my child's job to You. Thank You for good, solid relationships that she will make at work. I pray that she will associate with good, godly influences, those that will encourage her and those she can encourage, sharpening each other's character.[1] Thank You, Lord, for causing her to submit to her employers, thus bringing about Your favor.[2] Let her be an example of You on her job — in word, attitude and actions.[3] When her boss or other employees see _____, may they see You through her. Let her light shine.[4] Use her on the job as an instrument for Your glory.

Thank You, Lord, that my daughter is developing into the best worker her employer has; that the favor You have bestowed upon my child is surrounding her like a shield.[5] In Jesus' name!

GOD'S WORD SAYS

1. "Praise the Lord, O my soul, and forget not all his benefits" (Ps. 103:2).

2. "The Lord is my shepherd, I shall not be in want" (Ps. 23:1).

3. "Bestowing wealth on those who love me and making their treasuries full" (Prov. 8:21).

4. "A good man leaves an inheritance for his children's children, but a sinner's wealth is stored up for the righteous" (Prov. 13:22).

5. "Misfortune pursues the sinner, but prosperity is the reward of the righteous" (Prov. 13:21).

6. "The righteous eat to their hearts' content, but the stomach of the wicked goes hungry" (Prov. 13:25).

7. "The house of the righteous contains great treasure, but the income of the wicked brings them trouble" (Prov. 15:6).

8. "For every animal of the forest is mine, and the cattle on a thousand hills" (Ps. 50:10).

9. "And without faith it is impossible to please God, because anyone who comes to him must believe that he exists and that he rewards those who earnestly seek him" (Heb. 11:6).

128
FINANCIAL INCREASE

Heavenly Father, thank You for such a great salvation that Jesus purchased for me on the cross and for all the benefits that come with Your salvation. I purpose within my heart that I will not forget any of them![1]

You are *Jehovah Jireh,* my child's provider. You are his Shepherd, and he shall not be in want for anything![2] Father, in Your Word You said You bestow wealth on those who love You, and You make their treasures full.[3] Thank You that You have stored up the wealth of the wicked as an inheritance for the just.[4] Prosperity belongs to my child.[5] He will eat until his heart is content.[6]

There is great treasure in the house of the righteous.[7] You, Father, own all the cattle on a thousand hills.[8] I speak financial increase over
_____'s life right now in Jesus' name!
I praise You that You are the rewarder of those who diligently seek You.[9] Thank You, Father, for the abundant blessings You have for my child this day.

GOD'S WORD SAYS

1. "The Lord is my shepherd, I shall not want" (Ps. 23:1, KJV).

2. "But seek first his kingdom and his righteousness, and all these things will be given to you as well" (Matt. 6:33).

3. "The lions may grow weak and hungry, but those who seek the Lord lack no good thing" (Ps. 34:10).

4. "Every good and perfect gift is from above, coming down from the Father of the heavenly lights, who does not change like shifting shadows" (James 1:17).

129

FINDING A JOB

Father, my child needs a job. I thank You that You are the good Shepherd, and we shall not want.[1] Therefore I'm asking You right now to open up the right doors for a good job for my child — not just any job but an effective job — a good paying job. May she find a job which will enable her to reach her full potential.

As I seek You and Your righteousness, You have promised all these things will be added unto us.[2] As I seek Your face for my child, I shall not lack any good thing.[3] You are the giver of every good and perfect gift.[4] Therefore a good job belongs to _____! I praise and thank You for it now. In Jesus' name!

God's Word Says

1. "And my God will meet all your needs according to his glorious riches in Christ Jesus" (Phil. 4:19).

2. "The thief comes only to steal and kill and destroy; I have come that they may have life, and have it to the full" (John 10:10).

3. "Men do not despise a thief if he steals to satisfy his hunger when he is starving. Yet if he is caught, he must pay sevenfold, though it costs him all the wealth of his house" (Prov. 6:30-31).

4. "Let us then approach the throne of grace with confidence, so that we may receive mercy and find grace to help us in our time of need" (Heb. 4:16).

5. "It is because of him that you are in Christ Jesus, who has become for us wisdom from God — that is, our righteousness, holiness and redemption" (1 Cor. 1:30).

6. "Praise be to the God and Father of our Lord Jesus Christ, who has blessed us in the heavenly realms with every spiritual blessing in Christ" (Eph. 1:3).

130
GETTING OUT OF DEBT

Dear Father, thank You for being our provider. Thank You, Lord, for supplying all our needs according to Your riches in glory.[1] The devil comes to steal, kill and destroy. But You, Lord, have come so we can have abundant life.[2] Therefore thank You for breaking the power of debt in _____'s life right now. I command the devil to return sevenfold everything that he has stolen from my child.[3] And in Jesus' name I declare by faith that my child is being delivered out of debt!

Father, You said in Your Word to come boldly unto the throne of grace to obtain help in time of need.[4] So I come before You today to obtain financial freedom upon my child's behalf. Thank You for giving him Your wisdom[5] and discipline to handle wisely his finances from this day forward. I stand upon Your Word, declaring that from this day onward he is blessed and is a blessing in Jesus' name![6]

GOD'S WORD SAYS

1. "Commit to the Lord whatever you do, and your plans will succeed" (Prov. 16:3).

2. "Be diligent in these matters; give yourself wholly to them, so that everyone may see your progress" (1 Tim. 4:15).

3. "The sluggard craves and gets nothing, but the desires of the diligent are fully satisfied" (Prov. 13:4).

4. "My son, if you accept my words and store up my commands within you, turning your ear to wisdom and applying your heart to understanding, and if you call out for insight and cry aloud for understanding, and if you look for it as for silver and search for it as for hidden treasure, then you will understand the fear of the Lord and find the knowledge of God. For the Lord gives wisdom, and from his mouth come knowledge and understanding" (Prov. 2:1-6).

5. "Diligent hands will rule, but laziness ends in slave labor...The lazy man does not roast his game, but the diligent man prizes his possessions" (Prov. 12:24,27).

6. "I press on toward the goal to win the prize for which God has called me heavenward in Christ Jesus" (Phil. 3:14).

131
GOAL SETTING

Heavenly Father, thank You for the plans and calling You have for my child. I ask You to give my daughter insight to these plans. Cause her to commit them to You, for You have promised that they will succeed.[1]

As _____ begins to set goals for the future, I ask You to give her diligence to pursue these plans with her whole heart.[2] Thank You that the desires of the diligent will be fully satisfied.[3] Teach her to use wisdom in every area, and give her understanding.[4]

Thank You, Father, that she will not become lazy[5] but will be determined to set and meet every goal You place in her heart. Burn Your passion in her; that she shall press toward the mark for the prize of the high calling of God.[6] Thank You for causing my child to be a goal setter and a goal meeter. In Jesus' name!

God's Word Says

1. "Diligent hands will rule, but laziness ends in slave labor" (Prov. 12:24).

2. "Lazy hands make a man poor, but diligent hands bring wealth" (Prov. 10:4).

3. "All the nations you have made will come and worship before you, O Lord; they will bring glory to your name" (Ps. 86:9).

4. "I will praise you, O Lord my God, with all my heart; I will glorify your name forever" (Ps. 86:12).

5. "Commit to the Lord whatever you do, and your plans will succeed" (Prov. 16:3).

6. "If you remain in me and my words remain in you, ask whatever you wish, and it will be given you" (John 15:7).

7. "Don't let anyone look down on you because you are young, but set an example for the believers in speech, in life, in love, in faith and in purity" (1 Tim. 4:12).

8. "I am not saying this because I am in need, for I have learned to be content whatever the circumstances" (Phil. 4:11).

9. "Turning your ear to wisdom and applying your heart to understanding, and if you call out for insight and cry aloud for understanding, and if you look for it as for silver and search for it as for hidden treasure, then you will understand the fear of the Lord and find the knowledge of God. For the Lord gives wisdom, and from his mouth come knowledge and understanding. He holds victory in store for the upright, he is a shield to those whose walk is blameless" (Prov. 2:2-7).

132
GOOD WORK HABITS

Heavenly Father, I come before You today to lift up
_____ 's work habits to You. Thank You for causing my
child to be hardworking.[1] My son is not lazy but is diligent
in all that he does.[2] I pray, Lord, that in everything he is a
doer and not just a hearer or talker. Thank You that he will
bring glory to You.[3] Burn Your passion in his spirit, causing
him to work with all his heart.[4] May he give himself entirely
to the work You have called him to do.
Everything he does will be committed
to You, and his plans will succeed.[5]
My son is successful because Your Word
is remaining in him,[6] in Jesus' name!

Father, let my child be an example
to others.[7] Let his good work habits
rub off on those around him. I pray
that he will work with the right attitude and a good heart.[8] Cause him to
be disciplined in all he does so that discipline will be a way of life for him.[9] In Jesus' name.

GOD'S WORD SAYS

1. "If the Lord delights in a man's way, he makes his steps firm" (Ps. 37:23).

2. "Since you are my rock and my fortress, for the sake of your name lead and guide me" (Ps. 31:3).

3. "Go near and listen to all that the Lord our God says. Then tell us whatever the Lord our God tells you. We will listen and obey" (Deut. 5:27).

4. "And you, my son Solomon, acknowledge the God of your father, and serve him with wholehearted devotion and with a willing mind, for the Lord searches every heart and understands every motive behind the thoughts. If you seek him, he will be found by you; but if you forsake him, he will reject you forever" (1 Chr. 28:9).

5. "And with your feet fitted with the readiness that comes from the gospel of peace" (Eph. 6:15).

6. "Since you are my rock and my fortress, for the sake of your name lead and guide me" (Ps. 31:3).

7. "You guide me with your counsel, and afterward you will take me into glory" (Ps. 73:24).

8. "No, in all these things we are more than conquerors through him who loved us" (Rom. 8:37).

133

PREPARING FOR THE FUTURE

Heavenly Father, I come before You today to praise You for my child, _____. Help her take the right steps as she prepares for the future. Thank You that You are the one who is ordering her steps[1] and leading and guiding her in the way she should go.[2] I pray that she will listen to Your voice and obey it.[3]

I ask that she will prepare herself for the future by spending time in Your Word and in prayer.[4] Just as our feet are shod with the preparation of the gospel of peace,[5] so prepare my child's spirit, soul and body for the task You have laid before her. Thank You, Father, for You are her rock and fortress, the one who leads and guides her into all truth.[6] Thank You for guiding her with Your counsel.[7] My child is more than a conqueror, with victory and success in her future![8] In Jesus' name!

God's Word Says

1. "For attaining wisdom and discipline; for understanding words of insight; for acquiring a disciplined and prudent life, doing what is right and just and fair; for giving prudence to the simple, knowledge and discretion to the young — let the wise listen and add to their learning, and let the discerning get guidance — for understanding proverbs and parables, the sayings and riddles of the wise. The fear of the Lord is the beginning of knowledge, but fools despise wisdom and discipline" (Prov. 1:2-7).

2. "As for you, the anointing you received from him remains in you, and you do not need anyone to teach you. But as his anointing teaches you about all things and as that anointing is real, not counterfeit — just as it has taught you, remain in him" (1 John 2:27).

3. "If the Lord delights in a man's way, he makes his steps firm" (Ps. 37:23).

4. "But seek first his kingdom and his righteousness, and all these things will be given to you as well" (Matt. 6:33).

5. "'Honor your father and mother' — which is the first commandment with a promise" (Eph. 6:2).

6. "Let us not give up meeting together, as some are in the habit of doing, but let us encourage one another — and all the more as you see the Day approaching" (Heb. 10:25).

7. "Do not be misled: 'Bad company corrupts good character'" (1 Cor. 15:33).

8. "But you, dear friends, build yourselves up in your most holy faith and pray in the Holy Spirit" (Jude 20).

134
SETTING PRIORITIES

Dear heavenly Father, thank You for helping my child set his priorities. I pray that my child uses Your wisdom in all things.[1]

I release Your anointing to lead and guide him in the way he should go.[2] Your Spirit is helping him to prioritize his life, for his steps are ordered by You.[3] I ask that my child will put You first in everything he does. Let him seek You and Your righteousness.[4] I pray that he will respect those over him, honoring me as a parent[5] and remembering our family.

Help him stay plugged into Your Word and to the church.[6] I pray that he will associate with the right group of people, choosing his friends wisely.[7] Thank You for helping my child to build himself up in You above all things.[8]

Thank You, Father, because _____ is setting his priorities according to Your Word. In Jesus' name!

God's Word Says

1. "There is a time for everything, and a season for every activity under heaven" (Eccl. 3:1).

2. "Nehemiah said, 'Go and enjoy choice food and sweet drinks, and send some to those who have nothing prepared. This day is sacred to our Lord. Do not grieve, for the joy of the Lord is your strength'" (Neh. 8:10).

3. "Look to the Lord and his strength; seek his face always" (1 Chr. 16:11).

4. "Making the most of every opportunity, because the days are evil" (Eph. 5:16).

5. "Submit yourselves, then, to God. Resist the devil, and he will flee from you" (James 4:7).

6. "His master replied, 'Well done, good and faithful servant! You have been faithful with a few things; I will put you in charge of many things. Come and share your master's happiness!'" (Matt. 25:23).

135
TIME MANAGEMENT

Heavenly Father, thank You for giving me the opportunity to be the parent of _____. I come before You today to lift her up in prayer. I pray that she will manage her time wisely.[1] Fill her up with Your joy and strength.[2] Give her wisdom to make the right decisions. I pray that she will not get so busy that she burns herself out.

Most importantly help _____ to make time for You. In fact, I pray that she will seek You above all things,[3] making You number one in her life. Give her supernatural wisdom to make the most out of her time.[4] I pray that my daughter will learn to put aside the things that don't matter and will focus on the important things. I take authority over the enemy who would try to come in and steal my child's time and attention![5] Thank You that she will be a good steward of the time You have given her.[6] In Jesus' name.

God's Word Says

1. "And afterward, I will pour out my Spirit on all people. Your sons and daughters will prophesy, your old men will dream dreams, your young men will see visions" (Joel 2:28).

2. "Where there is no vision, the people perish: but he that keepeth the law, happy is he" (Prov. 29:18, KJV).

3. "Then the Lord replied: 'Write down the revelation and make it plain on tablets so that a herald may run with it'" (Hab. 2:2).

4. "The one who calls you is faithful and he will do it" (1 Thess. 5:24).

5. "Do not conform any longer to the pattern of this world, but be transformed by the renewing of your mind. Then you will be able to test and approve what God's will is — his good, pleasing and perfect will" (Rom. 12:2).

6. "Let us fix our eyes on Jesus, the author and perfecter of our faith, who for the joy set before him endured the cross, scorning its shame, and sat down at the right hand of the throne of God" (Heb. 12:2).

136
VISION

Dear heavenly Father, You have promised to pour Your Spirit upon all flesh in these last days. You promised that You would cause the young people to see visions,[1] for without Your vision people perish[2] and run wild. Thank You for giving _____ Your vision for his life. I pray, Father, that he will be obedient to Your Word and write that vision down so he can run with endurance.[3] May he not let anyone or anything get in the way of that vision.

Thank You, Lord, for equipping him to fulfill the work You have given him. May my child realize that You are faithful to do what You have promised.[4] I pray also, Lord, that my child will renew his mind in You so that he will be able to know Your good and perfect will.[5] May he never settle for second best but strive for the best with his eyes fixed on You and on the goal You have set before him.[6] Thank You, Jesus, for allowing my child to fulfill the vision You have placed in his heart.

CONCLUSION

You do not have to sit by and watch your teenagers self-destruct. No amount of psychological data can convince me that it's normal for teenagers to go through stages of rebellion and detachment just because of their ages. The Word says that young people are to "be an example to the believers in word, in conduct, in love, in spirit, in faith, in purity" (1 Tim. 4:12). God has bigger plans for our teenagers than we do! He has greater expectations of this generation than we could ever have! If we will commit to pray for the youth of this nation and the world, we will see the supernatural power of God turned loose to transform them right before our very eyes.

That means we have a job to do. The prayers in this book will help you use the Word of God boldly as you war in the heavenly realms for your teenagers (see Eph. 6:12). But prayers need to be mixed with faith in order to see results! Remember, Hebrews 6:12 tells us that we inherit the promises of God through faith and patience. Faith and patience characterize an active advance on the kingdom of darkness which realizes that "the weapons of our warfare are not carnal but mighty in God for pulling down strongholds"

(2 Cor. 10:4)! Do you really believe that God can move in revival on our young people? Then expect such a move! Throw away doubt and unbelief.

When the circumstances you see in your teenagers' lives seem to contradict the words you are praying, then choose to believe the Word. Isaiah 55:11 says that God's Word does not return to Him empty but will accomplish what He desires and achieve the purposes for which He sent it. Because you are praying the Word you can expect the results for which you are praying.

Remember, James 5:16 says that "the effective, fervent prayer of a righteous man avails much." Our intentional conversations with God can literally move His hand within our family's circumstances. If we will learn how to pray the Word, as parents we can see our families raised in the admonition of our mighty God and a generation completely changed into His image!

OTHER BOOKS BY EASTMAN CURTIS

Dare to Destinize
Turn Loose of Your But

AUDIOCASSETTES AVAILABLE

Saturated With God's Favor
Finding Your Vision
Great Big Joy
Armed and Dangerous
Force of Worship
Stir Up the Gift
Cutting Loose
Making a Difference

(each of the above titles is packaged
as a two-tape set)

VIDEOS AVAILABLE

Plugged In — Dare to Destinize
Plugged In — Outrageous Joy
Plugged In — Break Through to Victory

For more information on books, tapes or other products
or to obtain information about seminars
and conferences, please write or call:

Eastman Curtis Ministries
P. O. Box 470290
Tulsa, OK 74147
Phone: 918-250-3800